# THE LITTLE BOOK of
# BIG
# LEAGUE
# DREAMS

T.K. Lynn

Publication Date: 2018

Second Edition, 2019


©2019 T.K. Lynn, Parisio & Co LLC — All Rights Reserved

Published by Beacon Publishing House

Contact the Author(s):

Facebook: @LittleBookBigLeagueDreams

1. Sports 2. Baseball 3. Self Help

ISBN 978-1-7333951-0-6 (pbk : alk. Paper) PRINTED IN THE UNITED STATES OF AMERICA August 2019

*"No game in the world is as tidy
and dramatically neat as baseball,
with cause and effect, crime and punishment,
motive and result, so cleanly defined."*
— *Paul Gallico*

# Table of Contents

*"Let me win;*
*but if I cannot win,*
*let me be brave in the attempt."*
*— The Athlete's Oath*

I dedicate this book to my children,
Maddy and Marco.
"I love to watch you play."

*Much like all things in life...*

*BASEBALL*

*is a numbers game.*

*Nine Innings*

*Four Bases*

*Three Strikes*

*Two Teams*

*One Winner*

*"There is a story
behind every number,
on every back,
of every baseball player."*
*— Baseballism*

# PREFACE

The diamond pattern of a chain link fence is all that is between me and the game. I am an observer. Sitting on the sidelines and watching the art of play. Suck the salt off the shell of a sunflower seed, then pry open to enjoy the nut. Discreetly, or not, spit the shell. Game on.

It is a joy and an honor to provide this perspective about baseball and life lessons within baseball. Herein are reflections on basic how-to's of the game and some parallel life lessons.

It's been said that people can learn a lot from baseball if only they look close enough. I have looked long and hard while playing the game, watching the game, encouraging my children in their experiences of the game... and I have often used the game as a backdrop to explain life.

*"Learn how to overcome the failure*
*to meet the challenge."*
*— Danny Patterson*

In baseball, as in life, you have many opportunities to realize your full potential and make the impact in the world you're meant to make — in the moment.

Mirroring life, baseball is full of challenges. It's about how you show up, meet each and every challenge, and accept the outcome.

And, it is a game. Always a game.

*"The question isn't who's going to let me;*
*it's who's going to stop me."*
*— Ayn Rand*

Like planting seeds, ideas take root and then cross-pollinate from sports to work to education to family and etc. Some of the common themes I see from baseball and in life, I present as the CROPS cultivated here in this book:

**Confidence** — a feeling of self-assurance arising from appreciation of your abilities or qualities; believe in yourself and trust your work to bring results;

**Repetition** — a thing — like a training exercise — that is repeated, practiced over and over to build skills and learn by doing, reading, listening, pondering, and observing;

**Optimism** — confidence about the successful outcome; looking for solutions, finding opportunities in every challenge;

**Process** — a certain series of actions taken to achieve a particular end; don't get tied up in the outcome, results are feedback along the way;

**Success** — the accomplishment of a goal; failure is an element of success, if you don't fail, you're not pushing out of your comfort zone.

This collection of cultivated, curated, and considered information takes a look at some of the basic fundamentals of baseball, and at some fundamentals of life. With this, whether you play the game, coach the game, or are a fan of the game, my desire is that, by reading this book, you will have a perspective that will enrich your enjoyment... of the game and in your life.

*"Every day is a new opportunity.*
*You can build on yesterday's success*
*or put its failures behind and start over again.*
*That's the way life is, with a new game every day,*
*and that's the way baseball is. "*
*— Bob Feller*

For inspiration, you'll find quotes throughout this handbook that resonate across the years of baseball history. Also, it is an honor to interview and include echoing sentiments and wisdom of recently retired players who make their living training future generations to play the game.

In each chapter, there are tips for athletes, parents, and coaches to ponder — all in the name of enjoying the game. Many of these tips can be applied not only to baseball, but also to school, work, relationships, and other areas of life.

Whatever role you take on — player, coach, fan — your team needs you. The world needs you. It needs that special thing you've been dreaming of doing. In whatever you do, like in baseball, bring your A-game to positively impact people, organizations, and community. Make the best possible impression.

We all desire to live an extraordinary life — to be like a Pro! Often, professional athletes become icons, celebrities.

Through them, we vicariously, or indirectly, experience our dreams and our disappointments. We watch them experience victory and defeat at the highest level of competition in their field. And, through them, we experience it, too.

Whatever you do in life, bring your A-game. Chase your dream. Do your best every day. Then, get better. And if you get to play ball for your career, enjoy the experience. And if you don't get to play for your career, enjoy the experience.

The game of baseball is a lot about being in the right place at the right time. It is about getting the right bounce, and it is about getting the wrong bounce. Either way, it requires responding in the moment with the best of you. It is about getting into pressure-filled situations and having to play it out. Just like life.

Go after your goals with tenacity, courage, and determination. Persevere! Make up your mind about what you desire. Give little attention to the obstacles, keep sharp focus on opportunities, and have absolute resolve. Then, with every resource available to you, work to achieve your goal. And have fun doing it. That is the game of life and that is the game of baseball.

You cannot control what happens in the baseball diamond, you can control how you respond to it. That's baseball. That's life.

*"You cannot control the behavior of others,*
*but you can always choose how you respond to it."*
*— Roy T. Bennett*

*"Baseball is religion without the mischief."*
*— Thomas Boswell*

*"You can't second-guess baseball.*
*You can't second-guess yourself."*
*— Mariano Rivera*

*"To the people out there, baseball is a simple sport.*
*But it is complex. It is never easy."*
*— Dave Winfield*

# THANKS

With gratitude to the Little League coaches who give their time to teach the game to children and, sometimes, even to the players' parents.

To the club coaches who take athletes to the next level. To the school coaches who give lessons in the field of life and baseball. To the professional coaches who make a life of the sport of baseball.

And, especially, to every player who brings the game to life.

Special thanks for encouragement, contribution, and guidance from some of my favorite pro players, coaches, and trainers (in alphabetical order):

**Cameron Bayne**, former MLB pitcher and now a pro-style trainer at FieldFitGym.com.

**Drew Beuerlein**, former MLB Catcher & 1B now trains pro style fitness at FieldFitGym.com, author of *"Catching Grace, Understanding God's Grace in Everyday Life."*

**Ryan Buch**, former MLB Pitcher now owner and trainer at FieldFitGym.com, providing professional style agility and fitness training for athletes, one-on-one and one-on-some, assisting them in getting to the next level of physical ability.

**Cindy Larson**, trainer, coach, NASM — CPT, PES, CES, providing personal training, group training, and coaching for various league sports through high school level.

**Jorge Minyety**, former MLB 2B (also played Shortstop, 3B) and switch hitter, now coaches club team baseball, and provides individual fielding and hitting lessons as well as clinics. He is the Head coordinator of the OCOA baseball program.

**Danny Patterson**, former MLB Pitcher now coaches club team baseball, and provides private training for pitchers.

**Sundrendy Windster**, former MLB hitter and outfielder, now coaching club team baseball, and providing private training for hitting and fielding.

*"There are only five things you can do in baseball:
run, throw, catch, hit and hit with power."*
*— Leo Durocher*

*"They throw the ball, I hit it.
They hit the ball, I catch it."*
*— Willie Mays*

*"Baseball is the only sport I know
that when you're on offense,
the other team controls the ball."*
*— Ken Harrelson*

# ONE: BASEBALL

The baseball field is a diamond and, well, more like a series of them. Squares within a square actually. And we look at that square from the corners. So, a diamond. With curves, too.

Like life. It's all about perspective.

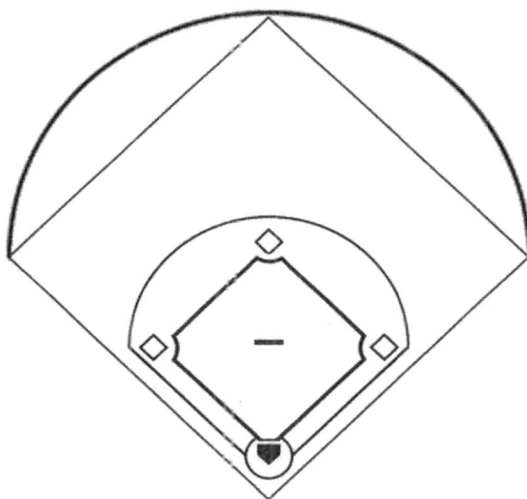

*"Become a student of the game, don't just play it."*
*— Danny Patterson*

In baseball, just as in life, whether you are an observing fan or an encouraging coach or a participating player, there is much to learn.

Former MLB pitcher Danry Patterson urges every and any player, regardless of position, to become a student of the game. Pay attention to the details. If you aren't clear about what they are or if you're not sure what's happening, ask! Be curious about every aspect of the game. Especially if you are fortunate enough to have a coach that has played at a higher than high-school level.

"NEVER think you know it all," Patterson advises, "I played this game until I was 34, and today, I'm still learning." The game changes with each generation. New strategies, new or improved ways of throwing, new technology, advance equipment, etc., all impact how the game is played.

So, in baseball, as in life, you will likely never know everything about anything. And, it is important to realize that you may know even less than others expect you to know.

As a coach or as a teammate, never assume that every player knows certain things. Every person has their own set of experiences. Rather repeat basics for all teammates than miss them for one player.

---

*A T-BALL TALE: At four years old, he had just moved to a new town and was signing up for preschool. One of the parents, a little league coach, invited him to join the t-ball team. The season had already started, so his first event was a game.*

*Having played whiffle ball with mom and dad, he had an idea about the game of baseball. What an exciting chance to meet some friends and play.*

*It was his turn. In his tennis shoes and blue jeans, he donned the batting helmet and stepped into the batter's box. The whiffle ball was settled on the tee. He swung and hit it over the heads of the players in the outfield who started to swarm in a chase to field it. And he stood there with a big smile on his face, watching them.*

*RUN! Go to first base! RUN! The crowd hollered. He couldn't understand why they were yelling at him.*

*He glanced about as panic set in. Then he marched off the field, tossed aside the batting helmet, and sat down on the makeshift bench saying, "I don't want to play anymore," as mom ran up to get attention of the coach. "He has never run the bases — he doesn't know about that," she realized.*

*With a bit of consoling and coaxing from mom, the coach escorted him back on the field and told him the secret next step. After you hit the ball, you run around the bases.*

If you begin playing T-Ball then move through league baseball, a typical developing team will have 12-14 players, depending on the age and stage of players.

The athlete will move through stages of development from having fun, to learning technical aspects, to the competitive arena, on to mastery after high school. Great coaches keep joy alive through all stages. Then, players learn to love the game while they learn to play it.

That is important in baseball... and in life. When you do what you love, the effort becomes a labor of love. And, following that passion will lead you to experiences of purposefulness. In life, and in baseball, you may play many roles. That is part of the fun.

Your role doesn't define you; it is just one of the ways to experience the game. For instance, a shortstop — and every defensive player — becomes a batter. In each role, you bring a perspective and a set of skills to the experience.

As the saying goes, "a person of many hats," is another way to describe the changing roles one may experience. When in the field at shortstop, a player wears the team hat. Then, when on offense, the same player puts on a batting helmet before the ump calls "batter up!"

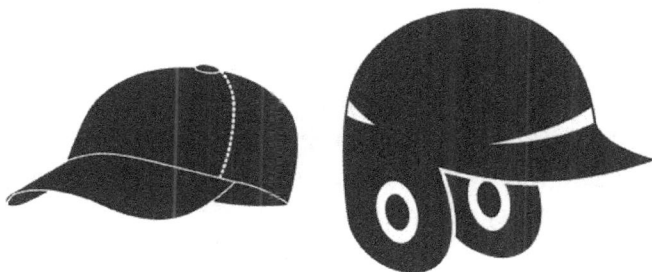

When the team is on offense, they are hitting. Usually developmental teams will rotate all players in the batting order.

When the team is on defense, there are nine defensive positions in baseball, so players are often rotated based on what the coach determines best for the team — and the players — in each particular game. It is good for athletes to play every position in the early years. And, as players develop, they will specialize and play more tailored positions.

Every player benefits from having some experience and understanding of every position. It is a helpful perspective for the game overall. Knowing the options will help clarify passion and purpose.

So, that is the general view of the game. Like anything in life, there is a playing field, there are players, and there are goals for engagement in the experience. Have fun getting to know the forest, and the trees — the ballpark and the intricate plays.

---

**player tip** - Inquire and investigate. Get clarity. If you don't understand something, ask questions! In baseball and in life, this is an essential, proactive way to participate in your development. And never assume you know it. Better to learn it or hear it again than to miss a crucial detail. One of the secrets to learning is repetition.

So when you think you're hearing something again, listen closely to reinforce what you know and to find a new bit of insight to deepen your comprehension.

**coach tip** - "Don't assume what a player SHOULD know," advises Danny Patterson. "It's easy to think the kids we're coaching should know certain things by the time we have the pleasure of making them even better. Remember, players don't always come to us from coaches with true knowledge of the game." In the formative years, many coaches are volunteers, with varying levels experience. This affects the strength of the toolbox that each player builds along the way.

Among factors that affect player development, athletes who are out for injury may miss periods of learning. So, as with everything in life, repeat the basics. Even if you think they've heard it before, students learn with repetition. Rather repeat a lesson many times than to chance missing it.

**parent tip** - Yes, it is frustrating to reiterate requests and requirements for your athlete. And, it is often necessary. To build response rate — the responsiveness of your athlete, consider using praise/reward instead of criticism/punishment that often diminishes spirit and self- esteem.

One way to implement this is to have consequences rather than punishments. For instance, when your player doesn't have their gear ready to go on time, it causes you, and them, to be late arriving to the field — and then they have the consequence of running extra laps.

Let them know they have a choice. They can take charge and do their part to be on time, avoiding consequences of being late — or they can run laps.

*"We are our choices."*
*— Jean-Paul Sartre*

# HOME & AWAY

The home team is identified on the schedule by being listed last. For instance: AWAY TEAM at HOME TEAM. Before a game, the home team takes the dugout along the third base line and the away team is in the dugout along the first base line. The home team takes the field first and has the last at-bat.

# DEFENSE

Nine players take the field on defense. The goal of the defense is to get three outs, and to prevent the opponent from scoring runs.

When your team is in the field on defense, each position has an associated number (not the number on your uniform) used to score putouts and to call out plays.

1. Pitcher

2. Catcher

3. First Base

4. Second Base

5. Third Base

6. Short Stop

7. Left Field

8. Center Field

9. Right Field

Whether you're a fan or a player, get familiar with these numbers! And, players, assist your teammates in knowing them, too.

## PLAYING BY THE NUMERS

So, here is how the numbers might come into play. In a game, if the second baseman fields a ball and throws it to the first baseman resulting in the runner getting out, it is recorded as a 4-3 out.

In a practice, the coach might call out fielding a 5-3 then hit a grounder toward third base, expecting it to be fielded by the third baseman (player number 5) then thrown to first base (player number 3). This is how such a play would be scored, too.

In a double play where the shortstop (player number 6) fields the ball and throws it to the second baseman (player number 4) who touches or steps on the bag then throws it to the first baseman (player number 3) who tags the bag for the outs, this would be recorded as a 6-4-3 double play.

Every position is essential to the game, just as in life — every role is important to the whole.

## OFFENSE

On the offense, all players become hitters and take their turns at bat with a goal of getting on base and advancing home to score.

Depending on the league of play, and coaches' discretion, all players might be featured in the hitting lineup or only the nine defense players included in the rotation. If only defensive position players are on the roster, they are typically substituted on the field and in the lineup.

In the lineup, hitters are often positioned strategically. The fourth hitter is sometimes referred to as the Cleanup Hitter and is usually a power hitter. This strategy plans that the first three hitters get on base and the fourth one drives in the runs (or "cleans up the bases"). A so-called "weak hitter" could be a speedy player who is very good at getting on base. There might be an opportunity for a great bunt—even a sacrifice—that would move on-base teammates forward.

It is all about working together to get on base. Then advancing baserunners to home for a score.

*"Good pitching will beat good hitting any time, and vice versa."*
*— Bob Veale*

As a player, regardless where you are in the batting order, your job is to get into the batting box and get on base. Within the overall game, there is a mini-challenge going on between the pitcher and the hitter. Know your count. Count on your instincts and your skills.

**player tip** - Own your experiences with the game. Be diverse. To find your favorite positions, learn them all. Be flexible. In baseball, as in life, the more you know about the field of play, the more you bring to the game. As the saying goes, see the forest and the trees. Play ball!

*"The great ones not only step up to challenges and find ways to overcomes them, they actually look forward to them."*
*— T. Jay Taylor*

**coach tip** - Remember that each player is an individual person. Find what makes each player tick — what motivates them and inspires them. Assist them in cultivating their passion and their talents based on their personal motivations.

Being empathically tuned into your athletes is a valuable and powerful tool for a coach (and for any leadership role in life). Take the time to figure out what your athletes are going through and where they're coming from, and you will instantly become more effective with them.

Look at each athlete individually, as an asset to the team, with understanding of the value that each player brings to the team. Assist the athlete in recognizing, respecting, and believing in their skills and abilities.

*"Don't teach with a 'blanket approach'*
*or you will produce 'cookie cutter' players."*
*— Drew Beuerlein*

**parent tip** - Encourage your athlete to play baseball and other sports till they find their passion. Then be available to work with them when they desire getting better.

The majority of players are done with sports by age 13. Often, they are not following their passion or there is interference from parents. Bruce Brown of Proactive Coaching advises that parents ask themselves the following questions before the first game:

1. Why do I want my child to play?

2. What do I think is a successful season?

3. What are my goals?

Then, ask your child the same questions. Are the answers the same? If not, then drop your goals and support theirs. Most important is the passion they have for the sport.

*"We were born with baseball in our blood.*
*It's more than just a sport. It's a passion.*
*It's an opera. It's just a way of being.*
*It's almost like breathing."*
*— Omar Minaya*

## CROPS

For consideration, and to further cultivate skills for life and for baseball, take a moment to nurture the seeds of success.

**Confidence**: be willing to do what you committed to do — even when you don't feel like it—and your dedication will fuel your certainty;

**Repetition**: repeating drills for the basics helps create, fine-tune, and reinforce muscle memory;

**Optimism**: be on the lookout for the "lucky break;"

**Process**: stay on task and in the moment, that is where the opportunity is

**Success**—define success as making the most of the moment.

# TWO: FIELDING

## NINE DEFENSIVE POSITIONS

Remember, when the team takes the field, it is on Defense. There are infinite things that can happen once you take the field. So, in baseball, thinking on your feet is as important as knowing the game well. This is true in life, too. Have an idea where you are going and be ready for surprises.

## OUTSTANDING IN THE FIELD

Always be ready. As the saying goes, keep on your toes! Actually, in sports, it is best to keep on the balls of your feet.

Bent knees and on the balls of your feet is the preferred ready position so you are poised to move. Being on your toes (the balls of your feet) keeps you alert and prepared to move. This stance is a tool that forces you to direct your attention and energy to what you are doing. Why do you think "on your toes" is such a popular idiom, or expression, in life? With that in mind, here are some of the key fielding possibilities.

**Fielding a ground ball** — When the ball is hit along the ground, it is a grounder. Be ready for a "bad bounce" as the ball travels the terrain. Watch it into the glove, scoop it up with your free hand and pull it in to your chest as you gain control of the ball.

The term "soft hands" is used when a player properly picks-up a ground ball with relaxed confidence, absorbing the momentum.

Keep an eye on the ball until you hold it solidly then step toward your target and make a good throw or tag out a runner.

**Fielding a tough bounce** — The ball may hit the ground in a manner that sends it off in an unexpected direction. This is another reason to keep your eye on the ball with laser focus and use your glove to get it. If it bounces wild and gets away from you, go after it and make the best of the play.

**Fielding a pop up** — A ball hit high in the air is a pop up. Let it fall into your mitt, don't reach up into it, but pull it down out of the air. Make sure you call it — alert nearby players that you will make the catch. "Got it!" This will call off other players who might be running in to make the play, avoiding a collision. If your teammate is in a better position to catch the pop up — and calls it — then back off and be ready to back up the play.

*"Field the ball like you're catching an egg;*
*if you're too rough, it's going to break,*
*so you must have soft hands and*
*watch the ball all the way into your glove."*
*— Sundrendy Windster*

**Fielding a line drive** — A line drive is hit hard in the air and has a low arc. Keep your eye on the ball. Let it hit the glove square in the pocket and hold on. If it takes a bounce, watch it all the way into your glove.

*"When you catch the ball, the brim of your hat should*
*be pointing to home plate. If it's pointing to the sky,*
*then you aren't tracking the ball*
*(this was told to me by the legendary Tony Phillps)."*
*— Sundrendy Windster*

**Fielding a fumble** — If you bobble the ball, stay with the play and complete it to the best of your ability. Keep considering the next best possible thing to do.

**player tip** - Once a play is over, it no longer exists. Let it go and prepare yourself for a brand new effort. The results are feedback. Use them to make any adjustments indicated. Then, get out of the outcome and get into the moment.

*"Never look back."*
*— Cameron Bayne*

**coach tip** - Never shame a player. Just as with all aspects of life, it is important to separate the behavior from the person. Every mistake is an opportunity to learn. This is especially important in developmental years when players are building self-esteem and confidence. Players are imprinting beliefs, perceptions, and paradigms. Give them nuggets.

Discipline is not about inducing guilt or even punishing. At any age, discipline is about correcting and guiding a person toward more appropriate behavior. It is about consequences.

So, instead of flying into a rage and yelling, ask your player "What happened?" Then, ask "What were the consequences?" And finally, "What can you learn from this?" Keep every experience productive. Start with a discussion.

**parent tip** - You reminded them to be focused. You reminded them to be alert. You reminded them to be smart. You reminded them to be tough. Now they know that. So, this time, just remind them to have fun, because sometimes they forget that part. It is, after all, a game. Play ball.

## LIFE TIP: DON'T FRET, DEAL WITH WORRY

Whatever you are contemplating, think about what will go right instead of what will go wrong. Find solutions for every possible pitfall — see yourself meeting challenges. Recognize obstacles and hazards, then focus on the outcome you desire rather than focusing on what bad could happen.

*"Don't borrow trouble."*
*— Cindy Kirby Larson*

Most of what we worry about never happens. And, when calamity does hit, usually it is more easily handled than we worried it would be. Show up in the moment and make the best possible move, minute by minute.

Another tool to thwart worry is to have supportive self- talk. Think about your strengths, what you did right, what you are learning. Congratulate yourself for attempting the task, for meeting the challenge.

Avoid beginning a statement with the words, "I had the worst..." or "I am so bad..." or "I suck..." and avoid thinking those thoughts. Instead, recognize your efforts with "I struggled..." and "I dared..." and "I ventured...."

When you find yourself worrying, distract yourself — either with a series of deep breaths, or with thinking that supports your success. Don't worry. Be happy.

*"My life has been filled with terrible misfortune;*
*most of which never happened."*
*— Michel de Montaigne*

## THE DIAMOND: FIELD OF PLAY

The baseball field is actually kind of a square that we look at from the corners. So, a diamond (image not to scale).

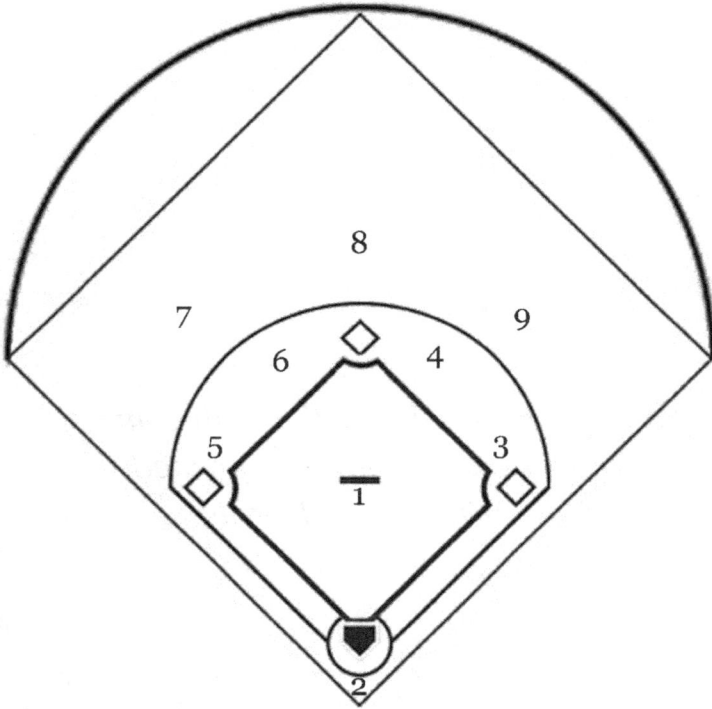

The nine players on the field are specialized in their positions. Like in life, every player is important to the game. Each one has a role and a talent to bring to the experience. And, remember, the role does not define the person. It just defines a perspective for the experience. Bring your best to the moment to meet the requirements of that role.

## THE BATTERY

On defense, the pitcher (player 1) and the catcher (player 2) have the most defined spots on the field. The pitcher is on the pitching mound in the center of the infield. The catcher crouches behind home plate. These two positions make up the battery.

The rest of the players have typical locations and can move most anywhere on the field. Players move around or shift depending on the batter (right or left-handed), the pitcher style, and the game situation. The coaches usually call movement on the field.

## THE INFIELDERS

Four players make up the infield: 1B, 2B, 3B, and SS (players 3,4,5, and 6, respectively). While there are typical spots for these players, they will shift depending on game situations.

1B: First baseman covers first base, most often playing just inside first base and a few feet back from the bag.

2B: Second baseman plays between first and second base, usually more towards second base.

3B: Third baseman covers third base, typically playing just inside third base and a few feet back from the bag.

SS: Shortstop plays between second and third base, usually more towards second base.

Both the shortstop and second baseman cover second base depending on the situation and where the ball is hit.

## THE OUTFIELDERS

Three positions make up the baseball outfield: LF, CF and RF (positions 7, 8, and 9, respectively).

Outfielders are responsible for catching fly balls, managing line drives, and fielding and returning grounders — running down baseballs that make it through the infield. They back up each other and they back up the infield. Good outfielders throw with both accuracy and velocity to the correct base or cut-off person.

Athletes in these positions will benefit from good speed, especially the Center Fielder.

CF: The center fielder requires speed and agility because they have more area of the field to cover.

LF: A lot of hits go to left field so left fielders require the ability to be strong defensive players.

RF: Right fielders require a strong arm to throw out runners going to third base or home plate.

In baseball, players play zone defense. This is similar to other sports, as well. When the ball enters your zone, it's your job to move to it and manage it.

---

**player tip** - Work on developing overall fitness plus specific strength and conditioning for the position(s) you desire. Physical work and mental development are both essential. So is rest.

Work hard. Play your best. Take time to rest.

**coach tip** - Encourage players to learn all positions, especially early on, so they become stronger in their specialization. And, keep things fun. It is, after all, a game.

**parent tip** - Reading is a great way for your athlete to relax. Inspire them with books about players, about baseball, about sports in general, and about other things they enjoy.

# RECOMMENDED READING

Here is a list of books that will enrich a player's experience of baseball and athletic skill building.

*The Mental Game of Baseball: A Guide to Peak Performance* by H.A. Dorfman and Karl Kuehl

*Heads-Up Baseball: Playing the Game One Pitch at a Time* by Tom Hanson and Ken Ravizza

*The Science of Hitting* by Ted Williams and John Underwood

*Tony Oliva: The Life and Times of a Minnesota Twins Legend* by Thom Henninger

*Harmon Killebrew: Ultimate Slugger by Steve Aschburne Pedro* by Pedro Martinez and Michael Silverman

*Pudge: The Biography of Carlton Fisk* by Doug Wilson

*I Never Had It Made: An Autobiography of Jackie Robinson* by Jackie Robinson and Alfred Duckett

*The Captain: The Journey of Derek Jeter by Ian O'Connor The Closer* by Mariano Rivera

*Unbroken: An Olympian's Journey from Airman to Castaway to Captive* by Laura Hillenbrand

*With Winning in Mind* by Larny Bassham

*Core Performance* by Mark Verstegen and Pete Williams

*"Athletes are born winners,
they're not born losers,
and the sooner you understand this,
the faster you can take on a winning attitude
and become successful in life."
— Charles R. Sledge, Jr.*

## THE POSITIONS

There are nine players who take the field. Each has a defined role. Each has a skill set that they bring to the game. Each has a role in supporting others. Like in life, every single player is uniquely important to the game.

All of us have bright futures ahead. If you don't hit your stride now, don't stress. You have plenty of time to get there. Just keep pushing to be better.

*"Being a professional*
*is doing the things you love to do,*
*on the days you don't feel like doing them."*
*— Julius Irving*

In baseball, as in life, you will have many roles to play. What is important is how you show up. Bring your best to the moment and then get better. Enjoy every experience and take away something from it to treasure. A nugget of comprehension, inspiration, or motivation. When you are standing in the field, be outstanding in your self.

# POSITION 1 — PITCHER (P)

Pitching gets more specialized as players develop in the ages and stages of baseball. Ultimately, there are three general categories of pitchers: Starting Pitcher (SP), Middle Reliever (ML), Closer (CL).

And pitchers can be defined by role: Ace, Starter, Relief Pitcher, Middle Relief, Long Reliever, Setup Pitcher, Closer, Left-handed Specialist, or by style: Power Pitcher, Control Pitcher, Ground Ball Pitcher, Fly Ball Pitcher, Switch Pitcher.

*"My pitching philosophy is simple:*
*Keep the ball away from the bat."*
*— Satchel Paige*

Regardless, the pitcher delivers the ball to the plate to start every play. Strong accurate throwing skills are critical for pitchers. For this, it is important to condition muscle groups that work together in the pitching motion.

Per Cindy Larson, NASM — CPT, PES, CES, a good conditioning exercise to assist core and more for pitchers is the side plank with dips. Hold the side plank position, then dip your hip to the floor and back. Change sides and repeat to keep your body balanced. Remember that it is essential to do exercises accurately. While this will assist every player with throwing skills, it is especially important for pitchers.

The pitcher and catcher start every play in their designated areas — the pitcher must be on the pitcher's mound with one foot in contact with the pitcher's rubber, and the catcher must be in the catcher's box behind home plate. The pitcher's job is to throw the ball over the plate in a way that it is difficult for the batter to hit, with the goal being to put out the batter by strike out, fly out, or force out.

The pitcher fields the ball on bunts, grounders, and pop ups, and backs up the catcher on plays at the plate. The pitcher will also back up base players depending on how the ball is put into play and who's on base.

This athlete trains for catching pop flies, grabbing line drives, and charging to field bunts or dribblers. Pitchers act as back-up on plays at home plate, and at the bases when a situation demands it. The pitcher will cover first base when the first baseman is fielding a ball hit to the right side; or cover third base when there is a throw from the outfield to 3B.

*PITCHER'S TIP: Get A Grip. From former MLB pitcher Ryan Buch, here is a fun exercise for pitchers. Place the baseball in your throwing hand. If you are standing, extend your arm behind you (you can also do this at night before sleeping — with eyes closed). Spin the ball in your fingers and find the seams. Without looking, grip the ball for different pitches: four-seam fastball, two-seam fastball, split-finger fastball, three-finger changeup, circle changeup, curveball, knuckleball, palmball, splitter, slider, etc. This assists your ability to get set for any pitch called, and your stealth in doing so while reducing possible tip- offs to the hitter from your movements.*

A pitcher must learn to manage the ball. When you can throw your fastball where you want it to go, you'll be successful. The mechanics of balance, finish, and follow-through are important. So is getting a feel for the grip.

The grip changes how the ball travels. Grip and release point affect the baseball's motion as it travels because the baseball has raised seams. Air resistance with the seams plays a role in the motion of the baseball.

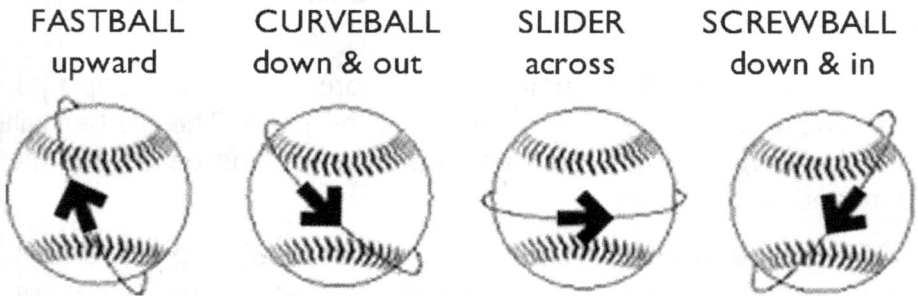

| FASTBALL | CURVEBALL | SLIDER | SCREWBALL |
|---|---|---|---|
| upward | down & out | across | down & in |

*"Keep the highs and the lows in the middle."*
*— Austin Reed*

A pitcher develops the ability to throw a variety of pitches — fast ball, change up, sinker, etc., with control of the ball. After seeing a few fastballs, the batter will usually get a sense of timing. That's when a change-up pitch comes in handy to throw off the batter. Create surprise.

*"Hitting is timing; pitching is upsetting timing."*
*— Warren Spahn*

Remember, in baseball, as in life, every moment has its own spin — a curveball spins from top to bottom while a knuckleball has hardly any spin. Each pitch has a different spin because of how the player grips the ball relative to the seams.

To prevent injury, it is recommended that a pitcher limit use of the curveball till high school — a curveball spins from top to bottom. When you throw a curve, let it come naturally — don't overspin it. Sliders challenge batters because they're faster and break much later than curveballs, and sliders breaks laterally and down.

*"The slider is the best pitch in baseball."*
*— Ted Williams*

A strong pitcher is able to keep composure under pressure — such as throw strikes when behind in the count or not get rattled when there are people on base. Maintain control and rhythm.

*The most important pitch is the next one.*

It is key to focus on the process. This moment. Moment by moment, one pitch at a time. Even with a count of 3-0 (three balls and no strikes), a pitcher focused on the process of each pitch, can strike out the batter.

*On June 12, 1880, John Lee Richmond, pitcher for the Worcester Ruby Legs, pitched the very first perfect game in baseball history.*

*"A hitter's impatience*
*is the pitcher's biggest advantage."*
*— Pete Rose*

## PREPARE TO PITCH

Pitcher preparation is key for getting to the next level. Professional pitchers spend more time preparing to pitch than actually pitching.

Develop leg strength. Strong legs assist a pitcher in generating velocity and maintaining stamina.

Fortify arms. Resistance exercises that are specially designed to improve arm strength, shoulders and back will assist pitching. Controlled long toss is an important training drill. Do it regularly.

Develop your range. Work on your mechanics. Then put the "spin" on it to improve your change-up and other pitches in your arsenal. Focus on getting ahead with first pitch strikes. Velocity or movement will up your odds of testing the batter.

*"I became a good pitcher when
I stopped trying to make them miss the ball
and started trying to make them hit it."
— Sandy Koufax*

Keep focus. If you get distracted, take a moment to regroup. Step off the mound, take a deep breath and refocus - then get back to work.

---

### SELF TALK & AFFIRMATIONS FOR PITCHERS

- *"I am a great pitcher."*

- *"When I don't get the results I desire, I learn from it and adjust for the next pitch."*

- *"I can do this."*

- *"When the result isn't what I desire, I learn from it and prepare for the next pitch."*

• *"This pitch is the one that matters."*

---

## EARNED RUN AVERAGE

A prominent, traditional baseball statistic for pitcher is the Earned Run Average, or ERA. It is defined as the number of earned runs (any runs that were not enabled by a fielding error or a passed ball) allowed per 9 innings pitched (or averaged over a regulation game). So, the pitcher is held especially accountable for earned runs, and responsibility for unearned runs (or errors) is shared with the team.

## WIN/LOSS

The pitcher is assigned the win or loss in each game, which is actually more representative of the team's defensive and offensive prowess or mastery. So, win/loss records are not always an accurate reflection of a pitcher's performance.

*"To a pitcher, a base hit is the perfect example of negative feedback."*
*— Steve Hovley*

## PITCH COUNT

Pitch count allowances increase with age and development. Still, there are many variables to keep in mind. As a player advances, it is important to condition ability to throw to the maximum allowed pitches — in practice and in games.

## BALK

The pitcher starts a pitch with his foot on the rubber on the mound. When attempting to put out a runner who is off the bag and ready to steal, switching pitching position from the windup, the pitcher must first properly disengage the rubber. While on the rubber, once the pitcher makes a motion associated with a pitch, the pitcher must complete the delivery or it is considered a balk and the base runners may be awarded a base.

**player tip** - Throwing Mechanics are critical. No amount of practice or exercises can combat poor mechanics. Constantly practice throwing in the correct manner to reduce stress on the arm and shoulder. Period. Perfect practice makes perfect.

*"Good pitches don't leave the ballpark."*
*— Aaron Sele*

**coach tip** - Ensure pitchers have good form to prevent injury, limit pitch count according to age and experience of the player, introduce more complex pitches as the player increases capabilities, and limit pitches that might stress growing joints.

Remind players that there will be good days, there will be tough days, and in-between days too. The pendulum will swing.

*"Baseball is a game of failure*
*so you're going to fail more than succeed.*
*You must be level minded day in and day out*
*— and enjoy the ride."*
*— Cameron Bayne*

**parent tip** - Make sure your pitcher is performing simple Baseball Pitching Injury Prevention Exercises every day — including getting adequate rest.

Consider working with a trainer to ensure proper technique. A trainer will assign specific exercises to support range of motion, muscular endurance, and strength, plus overall fitness to ensure that the pitcher is using the entire body correctly. High repetition of varied exercises is key to creating strong and healthy shoulder function. It is also important to make certain that there is overall balance in the body.

## LIFE TIP: INSPIRATION & MOTIVATION

### EMBRACE CHALLENGE

Work with people who challenge you. Someone a little better will push you to grow. No one ever regrets raising the bar.

*"The toughest competitors*
*will make you stronger."*
*— Josh Waitzkin*

### SEE PROGRESS

In recognizing your current skill level, you will see how far you've come, and you will honor what you have to do to get to the next level. Both benchmarks — how far you've come, how far you can go — are exciting. Let your past achievements and your future goals inspire and motivate you.

*"Achieving the extraordinary*
*is not a linear process."*
*— Christopher Sommer*

### MANAGE FEAR

Don't fear coming up short. The way to improve is to push yourself, find out exactly how far you can go, and take it to the next level. Recognize when you are experiencing fear — the emotion, the pattern, the result.

Reframe the events and the meanings you give things — everything is neutral until you give it meaning — for instance, rather than thinking "I'm not good enough" reappraise the situation and think "I am learning this skill." Release the emotions that hold back your success — redirect your focus and energy to serve you.

Respond to what is happening rather than reacting to it. With each incident, you can retrain yourself to let fear fuel you. Step into a new belief that serves your interests.

*"If something scares me,*
*there's magic on the other side."*
*— Kamal Ravika*

## POSITION 2 — CATCHER (C)

The catcher is like the conductor of the defense team. The players on the field are the instruments. This is the most critical position besides the pitcher. Catchers have a wide range of responsibilities requiring intelligence, tact, baseball sense, and leadership. Catchers are involved in every single play.

A catcher is rugged, aware, and quick-thinking. The catcher is more than a backstop catching pitches and blocking balls in the dirt, then returning the ball to the pitcher. This position is charged with signaling pitches, aligning the infield based on the situation, relaying plays, providing bunt coverage, blocking wild pitches, and throwing out runners attempting to steal.

*"A good catcher must be quick, but in control —*
*be a leader; control your emotions;*
*slow the game down."*
*— Drew Beuerlein*

A great conditioning exercise to assist catchers is squat jumps, per Cindy Larson, NASM — CPT, PES, CES. This exercise is good for building explosive power. It prepares muscles and joints of your lower body and will help increase your vertical jump. This is great for all players, especially catchers. To do this exercise, keep your feet under your shoulders and shift your hips back into a squat, as you power up, lift your arms straight in the air and jump as high as you can. As you land, return to a squat and repeat. With every exercise, it is important to learn good form in order to get maximum benefit and avoid injury.

## CALLING THE PITCH

With strategic direction from the coach, the catcher calls the pitch. This is where insight about the hitter comes into play. A seasoned catcher understands what type of hitter is up — tendencies, ability to hit a curveball, etc. Act with confidence. Take charge. Be vocal. This will give teammates confidence too.

**Common Pitch Signs** For basic pitches, the catcher signals the pitcher by putting down:

*One Finger = Fast Ball*

*Two Fingers = Curve Ball*

*Three Fingers = Slider*

*Four Fingers and/or Wiggle Fingers = Change Up*

The number of fingers for a certain pitch is arbitrary and can change. Just make sure you and your pitcher are aligned. When there is a pitcher change, make a quick visit to the mound after warm-up and confirm you are on the same page. With a runner on second base, be careful and disguise your signals so the runner cannot relay the pitch and/or location to the hitter.

## STICK IT

When the pitcher throws a strike, stick the pitch. The catcher's glove should not move in any direction except slightly back after catching the pitch. Briefly hold the pitch where caught, then throw it back to the pitcher. Sticking the strike is especially important for pitches low in the zone or with breaking balls.

## FRAMING

Framing is the art of making a pitch that is near the zone appear to be a strike when in fact it may not be — instead it is a borderline ball. A catcher who can frame well is extremely helpful to a pitcher who is working the corners of the plate.

## BLOCKING

One of the most important skills for a catcher to develop is the ability to block pitches in the dirt. Blocking is using whatever means available to knock down and control a pitch that bounces. Catchers who can block well prevent base runners from advancing on a get-away pitch. And, they instill confidence in their pitchers — a confident pitcher is a better pitcher.

## RECEIVING

Catching the ball is a primary skill for a catcher. A good catcher makes receiving look effortless. The basics is to have soft hands which is receiving the ball, not stopping it abruptly. Focus on absorbing the momentum of the ball.

Have soft hands, watch the pitch into the glove which should remain motionless unless the catcher decides to move it. Be quiet with the glove; be strong with the glove. Be patient. Let the pitch get to you!

## PROTECT THE UMPIRE

The catcher is a diplomat interacting with the umpire. Always do your best to protect the umpire from balls in the dirt.

## STANCE

There are two basic catcher stances and variations depending on the pitch or play.

**Relaxed:** Squat with feet shoulder-width apart. Keep hips and shoulders square to the pitcher and feet slightly staggered. Stay low and in a comfortable position. Relax mitt hand and point palm at the pitcher. Place throwing hand behind back. Present the pitcher with a good target.

**Ready:** When runners are on base or when there are two strikes on the batter, the catcher must be ready to block a wild pitch or quickly throw out a base runner. The ready stance is simply a raised squat with weight on the balls of your feet and bottom slightly raised. Keep hips and shoulders square to the pitcher, relax your receiving arm, and point your palm at the pitcher. Place your throwing hand in a fist behind your mitt. Present the pitcher with a good target.

Execute footwork determined by the pitch and throw back to the pitcher when the ball isn't h t.

## THROW DOWN

The catcher must develop a good throwing arm for the **throw down** at second. Once base stealing is permitted, a catcher requires the ability to throw out runners attempting a steal at second base. This play is timing dependent. To do this well, the catcher requires building the ability to get rid of the ball quickly — get maximum momentum while using minimal time — and throw with accuracy.

**Footwork** can make all the difference in throwing accurately. Foot positioning is key when getting ready to throw out a runner. A slight adjustment in your feet will give you a head start on your throw. Once you have control of the ball, use either load and throw, jump pivot, or drive to put it in play or return the ball to the pitcher.

**Load and throw:** Naturally come up out of the crouch during the step. Rock straight back away from 2B, then step forward directly at the target and release the ball. For the throw down, this takes overall strength.

**Jump pivot:** Once the ball gets to the glove, elevate off the ground just high enough to rotate the feet. Quickly turn the hips while both feet are in the air. When landing, the back foot will land just before the front foot, allowing you to drive off the backside on the throw. This assists a quick release than a high velocity throw.

**Drive:** For the most momentum on the throw to second, and just as quick as the pivot technique, once you have received the baseball, step forward a couple inches with the back foot. Square the hip with second base and complete the throw. Once you become more comfortable with this, you will be able to begin the step with the back foot forward and swing the hip almost simultaneously. This will allow you to cut down on release time.

**From the knees:** This throw takes advanced arm strength and ability. Catchers, and all players, benefit from practicing correct mechanics for this throw.

## LEADERSHIP

The catcher is the only player facing teammates. This position handles the pitcher, keeps track of the count (balls and strikes), and reminds players about the count and the number of outs. Leadership and confidence of the catcher can carry the team spirit and keep teammates aligned in strategy.

This position has insights to the opponent: Who's on deck? What pitch should be called next? Is the defense set? Where are the base runners? Are they fast? If the ball is hit to the gap where is the relay supposed to go? Is there a possible play at home?

With all of this insight, the catcher sets the defense. And, this player will back up first base on every infield play — if there is not a play at home.

**player tip** - To build your skill for accurate throw-downs, commit to practicing 10-15 throws over the distance from home plate to 2B using about 75 percent velocity every other day. And, accept the role as leader. Work on leadership skills. This will serve you well as catcher, and in other areas of life.

**coach tip** - Devote practice time to catchers — perhaps specific drills on the side. This will the result in fortifying a key defensive role. Work with your catchers to build insight and knowledge of the game. Teach them cues to understand hitters, and etc. Reinforce catching the ball and keeping it in the strike zone. Assist catchers in developing skills as leader.

**parent tip** - Work with your catcher, 3-4 times a week, making throws to second (on the field or over that distance if a diamond isn't available). Also find specialized training for your catcher. This role is filled with opportunities to engage physically and mentally. Support your athlete in every effort.

*"You have to have a catcher
because if you don't, you're likely to have
a lot of passed balls."*
*— Casey Stengel*

## CROPS

Dust up on the seeds of success. Build it. It will come.

**Confidence**: consider what will go right;

**Repetition**: get accustomed to operating under pressure so that, whatever you do, you will be more likely to advance even in the toughest situations;

**Optimism**: evaluate your options and choose the best one at the moment;

**Process**: know where you are going and take one-step at a time;

**Success**: recognize how far you've already progressed.

*"If you are accustomed to operating*
*under pressure to begin with,*
*you will be less likely to choke,*
*whatever you are doing."*
*— Sian Beilock*

## POSITION 3 — FIRST BASE (1B)

Each player has specific skills that help them excel at their specific position. The first baseman must handle short hops, make running catches on pop ups in foul territory, and throw the ball accurately when the pitcher covers first base.

*"I just go out there and do the best I can at baseball."*
*— Paul 'Goldy' Goldschmidt*

Like all infielders, the first baseman needs the ability to field ground balls. The first baseman needs to be able to stretch out, scoop the ball, and make picks (scoop errant throws out of the dirt) and catches to get put outs. This player fields this position, scooping up grounders hit down the line and tagging first for an out. First basemen must be alert, charge to field bunts, catch pop flies, and throw to other bases to catch a lead runner when possible.

An exercise that will assist first base players is the Superman exercise, recommends Cindy Larson. This movement targets muscles that help extend and flex your spine and neck and strengthen your core. It helps develop muscular strength and endurance in the spine.

To do the Superman, lay face down on a mat. Extend your arms and feet about shoulder's width apart. Then lift your legs and arms. Hold. Then relax. Repeat. You will feel a flex in your lower back. Lift, hold, and return to the starting position.

As with all exercises, it is essential to properly warmup before and stretch after doing the Superman. Learn proper technique so that you get the benefits and prevent injury.

There are a lot of throws to first base during a baseball game. The first baseman is potentially involved in nearly every play so must build ability to concentrate, focus, and keep their head in the game. Covering first base, the first baseman must catch balls thrown by other infielders for a put out.

*"Every day there is something new you are working on. It is a challenge every day and that is what makes this game so great."*
*— Anthony Rizzo*

First base is the perfect place for a left-handed player who can catch the ball well. And it is a perfect position for a right-handed player who can catch the ball well. Don't let anyone tell you what you can and cannot do — show them, and show yourself, what you can and cannot do. Then, do more.

**Stretch it**. Often, the first base player is required to reach for the ball while keeping a foot on the bag. So flexibility and agility is key to this position.

**Pick it.** Field throws from the infielders, whether they are accurate or not. Successfully fielding the short hop, whether it's a low throw or a ground ball to you, is a skill every player can develop. It is especially important for the first baseman. Your ability to scoop errant throws out of the dirt will give your teammates confidence that you have their back and will handle the short hop (a situation which usually results in an error for the player who threw the ball). Confidence will make infielders more bold and eager to go after the difficult plays to get the out, even if they run the risk of getting off a less-than-perfect throw.

**Get it.** Remain calm and watch the ball the whole way. Keep your foot on the bag and let your practice and ability take over. Get into position to make the play, then be aggressive with your glove. When in doubt, go get the ball.

In early years, the ball is often thrown overhead, bounced in the dirt, or off line. This is a great time to teach other players to back up first base. And to assist the first base athlete to stay focused on going after the ball, regardless of the pressure.

*"If you go to a game nervous, you make a mistake."*
*— Miguel Cabrera*

**Warm up.** The first baseman warms up the infield between innings by rolling grounders to the second baseman, shortstop, and third baseman. After they field the grounder, they throw the ball back to first base. This also gives the first baseman practice fielding throws.

Relax and trust your skills. Trust your instincts. Trust yourself and your teammates.

*"...if you're happy, you're more likely to have success."*
*— Paul 'Goldy' Goldschmidt*

**player tip** - Whatever position you play, you need to think many ways and make different moves to be one great player. Know the situation before every pitch. When you play first base, stretch to catch the ball when you can. Move to catch the ball when you must. And, once you are committed to playing first base, get a first base glove that will assist your play. Have fun out there!

*"I'm just trying to play my best and have fun."*
*— Miguel Cabrera*

**coach tip** - Consider your coaching style. Communicate in a way that will motivate and inspire players to work harder. Work to build confidence and self-esteem. Reinforce what your players are doing that works. Assist each athlete in learning exactly what they are doing incorrectly and show them adjustments they can make to fix it for the future.

*"Speak when you are angry*
*and you will give the best speech that you ever regret."*
*— Groucho Marx*

Lead by example. Show your team how to handle frustration around losing. It is important to lead by example and be a role model for your players. They are going to look up to you, and they will watch how you react to figure out what is acceptable behavior.

A coach with good sportsmanship will shake hands with the opponent and get the team ready for the game. The players will follow the coach's lead.

**parent tip** - Players know when they've made a mistake. Instead of lecturing them, take yourself out of the situation, step back and be the observer, let them work through it. Be supportive and encouraging. Once they realize by themselves that they made a mistake, they can take ownership of it, and they're less likely to repeat it. They will build their ability to manage "failure" and succeed.

# LIFE TIP: BUILD YOUR SELF ESTEEM

Self-esteem is learned when you are young and impressionable. Then it is reinforced throughout your childhood. Your beliefs are reinforced by parents, teachers, community, etc.

Every time you hear assessments, such as, "you're great at running!" or "you're terrible at throwing," you assume it's true! Then you move through life thinking "Ok, I'm good at running and bad at throwing." As you get older, these beliefs get fortified. You already "believe" you're bad at throwing, so you just avoid it. You'd rather be pitching. But you believe you are no good at throwing, so why try? To you, it's a fact.

But it isn't a fact. It's fiction. It is just a story you're subconsciously choosing to hold on to. It doesn't have to be permanent! Change the story.

Just as your taste buds change and develop over time, so does your body. Keep experimenting. Try a new position. And, even if it didn't work well at one time, try it again — something might have changed. Your body. Your skills. Your tastes. Your story.

Here is an exercise you can use to change the story and remind yourself that you are good, smart, capable, resourceful enough to reach your goals.

- Take deep breaths to calm yourself, when you're in a relaxed state, your mind opens to new ideas.
- Notice your current mental and emotional state.
- Recall a past accomplishment — big or small — and experience that moment when you felt a sense of mastery.
- Dwell on that feeling for a few moments.

When you focus on a feeling you experienced in the past, your brain feels it again. To feel confident, just reflect on a time when you felt confident.

This tool gives you a mental and emotional boost. It silences the annoying voice within that keeps telling you an outdated story.

With this technique, you can reinforce your belief that you can accomplish your goal. It will give you courage to give it a go. To work for it. And, over time, it makes you totally forget feelings of inadequacy. It gives you motivation and confidence to get out there and do it.

Sometimes, your brain forgets what you're capable of, so you just have to remind it every once in a while. Build your belief system so you have confidence and self-esteem to put yourself out there, motivated by your goal, without concern about how you'll be received.

# POSITION 4 — SECOND BASE (2B)

Speed, quickness, and good fielding ability are core strengths to build as a second baseman. This position requires adjustments based on the current situation.

A good exercise to assist this player is a squat hop with a turn, suggests Cindy Larson. This will improve acceleration or the ability to quickly go after the ball from ready position.

Stand with your feet shoulder width apart. Squat with your hips back like you are going to sit down, then jump up driving up into the air with your arms. While in the air you will turn around 180 degrees (a half spin) to face at your back. Land softly. Repeat 8-14 reps

For every exercise, it is important to warm up, practice with good form, and stretch afterwards, reminds Larson.

The second baseman fields batted balls and turns double plays. On a double play, when the ball is hit to the shortstop, the second baseman will cover second base, and vice versa. This player has the responsibility of covering second base on a stolen base attempt with the shortstop backing up the bag, and vice versa. Second baseman act as cut off point for the outfield when balls are hit to right field.

It is interesting to note that second basemen are typically right-handed; less than a handful of left handed throwing players have ever played second base in the major leagues. But then, like in life, some 'rules' are meant to be broken.

Knowing what to do when there are runners on base is a key opportunity for the second base player. It is also helpful to build the ability to get rid of the ball quickly.

A key strategy at second base is the double play. When the ball is hit to 2B with a runner on first, field the ball, touch second base or tag the runner, then pivot and throw to first.

The job of the player at 2B is to catch line drives or pop flies and field ground balls hit near that position. Then, the 2B player throws the ball to a base to force out a runner. If the runner is to be forced out at second base then that base is covered by the shortstop. On a hit to right field, the second baseman goes out toward the ball to act as cut-off for the relay.

The second baseman (and the shortstop) need to be expert fielders as lots of ground balls are usually hit to them during a baseball game — they must be aware of the strategic play based on the situation.

**DOUBLE PLAY:** a properly executed double play makes your team aggressive, fundamentally sound, and difficult to beat. When there is a runner on first, or runners on 1B and 2B, or when bases are loaded, the field is set up for a force out and the possibility of a double play. It is vital that the pivot player get to the bag early. The first throw to that player is the most important. The pivot player receives the ball, sweeps the bag, turns toe toward 1B and makes an accurate throw. Always step in the direction of your throw to assist accuracy.

**player tip** - A great second baseman can catch, throw, and field the ball well and they know the right place to be at the right time. You can learn this in practice and by observation. Know when to cover first base and second base, who to back up, and where to line up for cut-offs and relays.

**coach tip** - All infield baseball positions should be aware of how to play 2B. Share, teach and coach all players on the responsibilities and techniques on how to play 2B. Consider that all infielders benefit from the ability to play all infield positions, to be interchangeable and versatile.

**parent tip** - A fun way to work with your 2B athlete is by watching the pros. Notice and comment on all the ways the second baseman manages each play — fielding the ball, stopping the steal, communicating with the other players. Ask your player to explain all the ways to play 2B. This adds another method for learning the information and for repetition.

## CROPS

For consideration, and to further cultivate skills for life and for baseball, take a moment to nurture the seeds of success.

**Confidence**: have trust in your ability to persevere;

**Repetition**: master your skill set and get better at doing it, and a good way to do that is to doing the same correct thing over and over again; mastery is achieved through repetition... it is said that after 10,000 correct reps, an athlete is so fluid, making it look so easy that you think you could do it just watching them;

**Optimism**: be realistic about your situation and surroundings — false hope betrays you in the tough moments;

**Process**: see the big picture, make the next move;

**Success**: realize that you're just experiencing failure (which is always an element of success), you are not a failure.

## POSITION 5 — THIRD BASE

This position has the nickname **the hot corner** because of so many hard hit balls toward third. This athlete needs to have the quickest reflexes of any infielder because this position usually plays closest to the batter. Like all infielders, the third baseman must be agile and able to start and stop quickly.

*"It's almost like a cliché,*
*but we'll just prepare for nine innings of baseball*
*and not think about the past;*
*those things are done."*
*— Chipper Jones*

Cone drills are excellent conditioning for third base, and for all players, says Cindy Larson. Set up cones to guide various sprints, side shuffles, and backpedaling to build change-of-direction speed and agility. Cone drills teach multi-directional body position, body control, and body adjustment to dynamic forces during movement.

The player at third base fields batted balls, including bunts, on the left side of the infield, beyond the range of the shortstop.

The third baseman will field throws to third base on stolen base attempts and force-out opportunities. This player will also make running catches on pop ups in foul territory.

This position has the longest throw of all the infielders, so should develop a good arm. This player requires a strong, accurate arm to throw across the diamond to first base. Work on strength and accuracy of your throw. It is critical for third basemen to be ready for a hard hit ball in their direction since most right-handed hitters pull the ball, and left-hand hitters hit the ball down the line.

Trust your skill set. Know that you have laser-sharp focus and lighting speed reflexes.

*"I used to get hit in the cup at third, then I moved to shortstop and I never got hit in the cup. Then I moved back to third, and got hit in the cup again."*
*— Cal Ripken*

Like with other infielders, it is important that the 3B player know what to do in different situations. This player charges the ball on bunts and slow grounders. With a runner on second or third, 3B is the cut off and on a ball h : to left field.

Develop the ability to move side to side quickly the on balls hit hard down the line or to the left "in hole" between third and short.

*"It's a pretty sure thing that the player's bat is what speaks loudest when it's contract time, but there are moments when the glove has the last word."*
*— Brooks Robinson*

Historically, third base has had the lowest fielding percentage of any position. Panic is Bad. Preparation is key. With preparation, you can be comfortable enough to be calm and focused. Watch the ball all the way to your glove.

*In 1957, Frank Malzone received the first Gold Glove award for a third basemen in MLB history.*

Once you have control of the ball, step toward your target as you make the throw. Again, the third baseman needs to have a strong arm as it's a good distance from first to third base.

*"I don't think you appreciate everything that is happening in the moment. You need time to reflect."*
*— Ron Cey*

**player tip** - For playing 3B, work on your range so you can catch, or at least knock down, any ball hit in your direction. Be confident in your skills. Warm up and throw long toss to keep your arm ready to make the long throws from third base to first base.

**coach tip** - Remind your 3B player to stay focused, have soft hands, and to keep a relaxed body at all times. That will allow the most reflexive response to every play.

Balls hit toward third base are often harder hit than those going toward the middle of the field. Make sure your athlete is confident and has laser focus. This will assist overcoming fear and prepare them for alert agility.

**parent tip** - Do not undermine the coach in front of your athlete — no matter what the play. If you have differences with the coach (or with other players or their parents), take it up with the adults in private.

It is essential that the players respect for the coach (and for other adults) be upheld in order to maintain morale for the athletes and confidence in the team.

# POSITION 6 — SHORTSTOP (SS)

The shortstop will potentially field more ground balls, in more off-balance positions — and has more ground to cover than any other player. Shortstop must work on being quick, agile, and develop a strong throwing arm.

To prepare for this position, Cindy Larson suggests mountain climber twists. It is a total body workout that great for abs, the core, and it stabilizes the shoulder.

Get into push-up position (arms straight and balls of your feet on the floor). Brace your core to keep your body still and stable throughout the exercise. Keep your back neutral and your body balanced. Slowly lift your right knee up toward your left armpit, then back down again to the starting position (your feet only touch the floor when in the starting position).

The "twist" comes from your core and hips, not your shoulders. Repeat again with your left knee up to your right armpit, and alternate legs with each rep. Get a rhythm of steady breathing through the exercise.

*"Nobody ever won a pennant without a star shortstop."*
*— Leo Durocher*

The shortstop needs to think ahead to know where to go with the ball to make the play.

The shortstop has the same basic responsibilities as the second baseman, which are to field batted balls and turn double plays.

The shortstop covers second base on a double play when the ball is hit to the second baseman, and vice versa. One of the two players has the primary responsibility to cover second base on a stolen base attempt while the other backs up the bag.

When covering second base, get to the bag before the ball. Once you reach the bag, show a target for where you want the ball to be thrown. Once you receive the ball, get across the bag.

This player acts as a cut off for balls hit to left field.

## Receiving Positions for Shortstops

The key is to touch the bag on a force and avoid interfering with the runner.

**Receiving Position #1**: Outside of the bag (involves a throw from the third baseman) Call for the ball to be thrown to the outside of the bag. Step on the outside of the bag with the left foot, then make the throw to first.

**Receiving Position #2**: Inside of the bag (involves a throw from the second baseman that will take the shortstop to the inside part of the field). Call for the ball to be thrown to the inside of the bag. Once the ball is received, touch the base, then make the throw to first base.

**Receiving Position #3**: Take It Yourself (involves a chopping ground ball through the middle of the infield). The difficulty with this technique is that if it is not a hard hit ball, the baserunner on first might be right on top of you, so use the bag as protection from the baserunner. Field the ball, touch the back of the bag, and then make a good, strong throw from behind the bag. This will give you some cushion from the runner's position. Don't go across the bag or you risk colliding with the baserunner.

Keep your feet moving when fielding the ground ball. Watch the ball all the way into your glove. Use both hands to get control. Step into your throw.

Talk it up. The shortstop will often call out the play.

*"The most important thing is communication.*
*If we have the communication,*
*I think we could be good."*
*— Edgar Renteria*

**player tip** - You don't always need to practice fielding with a live ball. You can work on receiving positions and on receiving techniques without a ball. Grab your glove and shuffle, squat, scoop. A tennis ball or a waffle ball bounced in the house at short distances can build skills in a safe manner. Play.

**coach tip** - Make praise descriptive instead of generic. For example: Instead of a generic "good job!" say, "I like that you stayed with that play to the end!"

Ask players to analyze the r game. Always lead with what went well, find a "room to improve" morsel, and wrap up with a strength or encouragement.

Keep it encouraging. Instead of saying "don't drop the ball!," motivate your players when you say "hold on to the ball."

**parent tip** - To support se f-esteem and assist your athlete in learning from situations, ask your player What? questions: What happened? What was the consequence? What can you learn from this? Asking What? questions prompts reflection where asking Why? can result in defensiveness.

## OUTFIELD

Outfielders cover a lot of ground. They must work on the ability to catch fly balls above their head and on the run. They also will need to build the ability to throw the ball accurately, a long distance.

These players catch batted fly balls, field and return ground balls and line drives that make it through the infield, and back-up the infielders during plays at a base. Outfielders also back up one another.

Speed and quick reactions to the ball are important skills to develop. Good fielding requires a combination of mobility, speed, agility, and ball handling to make throws with both accuracy and velocity to the correct base or cut- off person.

---

*Speed is its own skill and must be trained. Running laps will not make you quick or fast, it will just make you fit. Laps will train endurance. Speed requires specific work. To run faster, you must train by running fast — sprinting — and by building twitch muscles. Speed is won back every season, and advanced from there. As you run fast and train fast, you get faster.*

---

Outfielders have a long view. When a ball is hit in the air toward them, they are instructed to take the first step back while assessing things.

This is a good skill for life. Chaos Theory suggests that if you step back far enough from anything, you can see the underlying order that is emerging there. Whether catching the ball or catching self-talk, step back. When your first thought is negative — what could go wrong? — change it to: what must I do to optimize outcome?

Stepping back builds awareness. It gives you that moment to see the big picture and make a choice that best serves you. Which way will you turn?

Then, here are a couple techniques for getting the ball back in the infield.

**The Crow Hop** - bring the ball to the throwing slot in a quick, controlled motion to generate forward momentum, hop one time and released the ball with a long hop.

**The Jump Step** - field the ball, bring the ball to the throwing slot in a quick, controlled motion while generating momentum towards the field. Field the ball with control, stride, stride and throw.

The key to both these techniques is to utilize momentum and body leverage to deliver a strong accurate throw. An outfielder on a "Do or Die" clutch play has a chance to get an assist. Footwork assists an outfielder in fielding the ball to achieve this goal.

**player tip** - As discussed, two throwing techniques that are key in clutch plays are the Crow Hop and the Jump Step. Get the footwork down and secure the assist.

Every day, set a clear goal for yourself. Clear daily goals are like rungs on the ladder of you journey to success. Goals keep you focused on what you desire to accomplish. Each day, experience a successful step toward the finish line. See progress. Every day.

**coach tip** - Teach players from early on to get into the "ready" position before every pitch: on the balls of their feet, with feet under shoulders, and with knees bent and ready to move.

Teach players to keep moving and to think about where the ball is going, what plays are possible, and how they will best serve the current situation.

Shout out the play, field the ball, be a relay point, run down a passed ball, and enjoy the game.

**parent tip** - Younger outfielders may find it difficult to concentrate on the game, since balls are not hit to the outfield as often as to the infield. Give them tips to assist their focus. And be patient.

## POSITION 7 — LEFT FIELD

Of all outfield positions, this player does not throw the ball as far as the center fielder or right fielder might.

To train for this position, a good focus is core strength. From planks to pushups, from sit-ups to superman, from mountain climbers and more, core exercises focus on the entire torso and the stabilizing muscles. To build solid core strength, mix it up to involve all the stabilizing muscle groups.

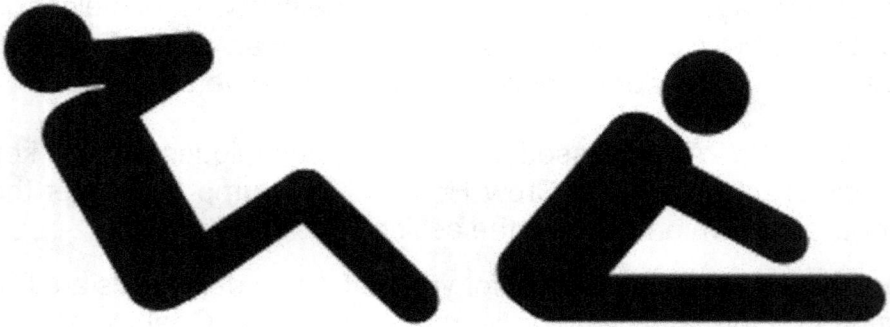

Like all offense positions, the left fielder requires good fielding and catching skills. Attack the baseball. Be aggressive and stay in control.

This player moves to back up third on pick-off attempts from the catcher or pitcher.

Every field player will benefit from learning to focus in the moment. This play. Then then next. Then then next. Mentally disregard the last play. Forget about it. The only thing that matters now is this play. Stay with it. Make it happen. Move on.

Sometimes, the biggest moments are the small ones. In baseball, and in life, it is all happening in the moment. Always look for greatness — it's there.

*WAR: Wins Above Replacement or Wins Above Replacement Player, commonly abbreviated to WAR or WARP is baseball statistic developed to sum up a player's total contributions to the team. A high WAR value built up by a player reflects successful performance, a large quantity of playing time, or both combined.*

**player tip** - You can strengthen your weaknesses. Embrace them and take time to concentrate on them. Working on these areas is how you build strength. As your skills add up, you can be even more proud of the work you are doing — let it motivate you to carry on.

Be the athlete you are today — and do the work to the best of your ability. Every day is an opportunity to learn more about yourself as an athlete. Don't fear getting out of your comfort zone.

**coach tip** - Being uncomfortable can be annoying and it is necessary to stretch and grow. Remind players that being uncomfortable is what it will take to develop a new skill and to get comfortable. Assist athletes in embracing the process of becoming the most extraordinary versions of themselves.

**parent tip** - Not every success can be measured. Encourage your athlete to see success in as many ways as possible. Remind them to look how far they've come in this journey. Thwart discouragement by reflecting on the payoff from their work. Motivate and inspire continued effort.

## POSITION 8 — CENTER FIELD

The athlete playing center field requires a combination of speed and throwing distance. This position player will cover more 'grass' than any other player and will likely catch the most fly balls.

To prepare for this position and build agility for side-to- side movement, Cindy Larson suggests Lateral A-Skips. Begin with a dynamic warm up. Then, skip by pushing off with your left leg and driving up your right knee. Then drive down your right foot as you skip and raise your left knee. Do not cross your legs or feet. Keep your hip, knee, and ankle aligned. Stay erect — do not slouch. Shuffle sideways as you continue skipping this way. Swing your arms to assist movement. This assists lateral movement and speed. Again, with every exercise, it is critical to use good form. Perfect practice...makes perfect.

The center fielder backs up second on bunts and throws from the catcher.

An important skill to develop is judging the ball on the fly. The center fielder must run to where the ball is going to be.

*"I skate to where the puck is going to be,
not where it has been."*
*— Wayne Gretzky*

Having a sense of how the ball moves and where it is going will develop over time.

---

**A PLAY TO REMEMBER:** *The Catch is one of the most memorable plays in the history of baseball. It refers to a defensive baseball play made by New York Giants center fielder Willie Mays on a ball hit over 460 feet into center field by Cleveland Indians batter Vic Wertz during Game 1 of the 1954 World Series, September 29, 1954. Mays was playing in shallow center field and made an on the run, over-the-shoulder catch on the warning track to make the out. Because of the difficulty of the play and the importance of the game, The Catch is one of the most memorable plays in baseball history.*

*Your body has never been in the exact same moment twice. It adjusts hundreds of times each day. You have the ability to respond to life as you choose. Every moment is a new world of opportunity. Don't let limitations define who you are.*

---

**player tip** - Practice. To improve in any skill, and to achieve mastery of that skill, repeat it 10,000 times correctly. Never miss a chance to improve. From complex fielding drills with teammates to throwing a tennis ball against a wall on your own to imagining and reflecting on good mechanics — continue to work on your skills. Build concentration and hand-eye coordination.

*"It is frequent repetition that
produces a natural tendency."*
*— Aristotle*

As a skill is practiced over time, the activity becomes easier and easier while becoming habitual and reflexive.

Persevere. Have fun chasing your dream. Enjoy every step, every challenge, every setback, every victory. Find the opportunities. Go get 'em.

**coach tip** - Throwing in the ball quickly and accurately from the outfield is an important skill for every fielder to master. Provide multiple drills to build and reinforce this behavior so it can become an almost automatic response.

**parent tip** - This is a tough sport. That challenge attracts your athlete, and it can discourage them. Remind your player that they accomplish something every time they step up to bat or into the field. That sense of accomplishment is what brings them back to the game every time. Encourage them to take a chance, to persevere.

## LIFE TIP

Fortify your ability for self-control by:

**Breathing.** Be mindful of your breath, breathe deeply and fully.

**Exercising.** Do something every day — a brisk walk, a jog, yoga, stretching; even on a scheduled rest day you can expand by meditating or thinking about your sport.

**Relaxing.** Avoid stress or combat it.

**Eating.** Consume adequate protein, complex carbohydrates, and good fats (coconut oil, avocados, butter, omega 3s, extra virgin olive oil).

**Sleeping.** Get enough good quality sleep.

*"I think it's very important to have a feedback loop where you're constantly thinking about what you've done and how you could be doing it better. I think that's the single best piece of advice: Constantly think about how you could be doing things better and questioning yourself."*
*— Elon Musk*

## CROPS

Attend to your growing skill set.

**Confidence**: build self-confidence with feedback loops to signal when you require adjustments that support your progress;

**Repetition**: muscles grow accustomed to certain types of movement, the more often you correctly do a certain activity, the more likely you are to do it as needed, when needed... and, it is critical to balance training with varied exercises (cross training) for the same outcome and proper rest for repair;

**Optimism**: find the most successful outcome in every situation;

**Process**: focus on your practice instead of performance, stick to the process so you enjoy the present moment and improve;

**Success**: release the need for immediate results, move on and stick to your process and continue to progress.

# POSITION 9 — RIGHT FIELD

Like all players, the right fielder needs to be able to think- ahead. Look at where offense is positioned on the bases. Is the batter left handed? If so, it is more likely the hit will pull to right field.

This player, like all of them, relies on core strength and power, and acceleration. Cindy Larson suggests push-up sprints, a drill that assists reaction time and acceleration. Begin in pushup position and thrust into a sprint. To make the drill more interesting, add the element of racing to beat your own time reaching the goal endpoint.

The right fielder backs up first base on all throws from the catcher and on bunted balls when the catcher must be available for fielding the ball. The right fielder also backs up second on any ball thrown from shortstop, third base or foul territory (left of the diamond).

---

*OUTSTANDING IN RIGHT FIELD: Right fielders historically have power bats and strong throwing arms. Among those with a cannon for an arm, speed in the field and on the bases, plus hitting for power and average are players like Babe Ruth, Frank Robinson, Hank Aaron, Mell Ott, Ichiro Suzuki,*

*Roberto Clemente, Reggie Jackson, and Ton Gwynn. These memorable athletes played the majority of their careers in right field.*

---

In baseball, as in life, don't look to your situation as if externals are to blame for holding you back. Instead, use disadvantage as a springboard for achievement. For every flaw, weakness, challenge one might use to remain stuck, someone else will use as an opportunity to succeed. Take responsibility for you; look for and find solutions.

---

**player tip** - Get fit. Good overall fitness means quicker reactions, stronger throws, and faster sprinting.

**coach tip** - Give your players drills to improve fielding technique, speed, and conditioning. Encourage them to do the drills a couple times each week all year long to be ready for the upcoming season. Consider adding a resistance band to improve lateral acceleration, increase range, and assist them to get to balls more quickly.

**parent tip** - Support your athlete in getting fit, overall. There are a variety of readily available exercise options from jogging in the park, doing pushups and pull-ups and planks, incorporating squats and lunges, etc., to get a full-body workout. Make it a family effort. Motivate with fun. Maybe even challenge one another to improve. Be sure to work within limits and push appropriately to be safe and injury free. And, definitely, before starting any regimen for your player, yourself, or your family, consult your physician.

# THREE: CATCHING THE BALL

Baseball fans love an epic catch. It pumps up the crowd with awe: "Did you see that?!" Climb the walls, reach over the fence, outrun the ball, dive for it, backhand it on the run, leap and grab it, and watch the ball into the glove. Great catches stop scoring, rob home runs, and impress all around.

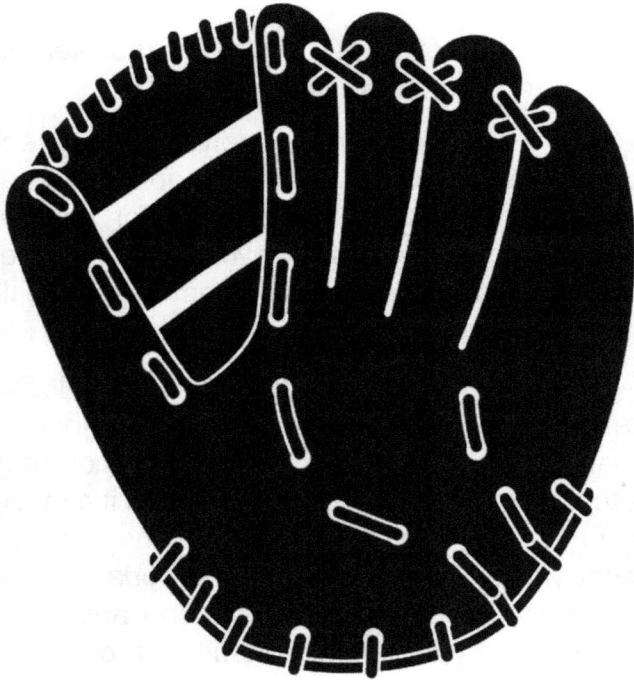

But first, catch the ball. With enough practice and determination, anyone can catch a baseball. Like with anything, it just takes practice and concentration. Begin with your stance and body position. Be in an athletic position to be ready to catch a ball.

## THE ATHLETIC POSITION

- Bend knees slightly to give you flexibility, prepare you to lunge for the ball, and assist your focus.

- Have your feet under your shoulders (if your base is too wide, you will have to rock out of position rather than burst from it).

- Squat slightly and hinge at the hips keeping a long, flat back.

- Keep shoulders toward the target so you can see and react once the ball comes to you.

- Stand on the balls of your feet instead of on your toes or heels or flat-footed.

The athletic position is key to every sport. From this stance, you are ready to burst into action.

Move to where the ball will be. Keep your feet moving so that, most of the time, you catch the ball in front of you.

---

**PRO STYLE:** *Ken Griffey Jr. was known his laid-back attitude, a powerful bat, and speed in the outfield. That speed helped him get to where the ball was going and make some great plays. He took home ten straight Gold Gloves from 1990-1999.*

---

If a throw is offline, or a hit is to the hole, quickly shuffle your feet in order to receive the ball with your glove in front of you. There will be times when you must reach out and snag a ball without moving to the side. Work to keep the baseball in front of you.

Catch the ball in the pocket, then close your glove to secure the ball. It's a good habit to catch the ball with two hands. If you catch with one hand, it is difficult to get rid of the ball in time. In any case, using two hands will help avoid drops until catching the ball feels easy and natural.

"Keep your eye on the ball" is one of the most commonly used phrases in baseball — and it is a metaphor for life. It is good advice for any aspect of the game, and for achieving your goals.

You can't catch what you can't see. And what you focus on, grows. So, in life, keeping your eye on the ball means staying aware of your goal — know the long-term desire and the steps necessary now to move toward that goal. And in baseball, know the field, where the opportunities are, and make the optimal play in the moment. The ball is in motion. Field the ball.

The most important part of catching the ball is watching the ball and tracking its flight path. It's about focus and judgment.

---

**PLAYER STAT:** *Add athleticism to the ability to catch the ball and you can make history. Andruw Jones was one of the best centerfielders in the game earning ten consecutive Gold Gloves from 1997-2007.*

---

Focus so you pick up sight of the baseball out of your teammates throwing hand or off the bat as soon as possible. Pay attention to speed and trajectory. Watch the ball all the way into your glove.

A common mistake that players make is to assume the catch and take their eyes off it a split-second too early, only to have the ball glance off the glove. Don't take your eyes off the ball until it is in your glove.

Have relaxed hands to catch the ball. Tension works against you. Instead of reaching for the ball, let it fall into your glove — pull it from the sky.

*"Catch the ball with soft hands."*
*— Sundrendy Windster*

Make the play and remember good sportsmanship. Manage your reaction post-play. No emotion, no flashiness, no nothing — just baseball purity. Feel it and move on. There is a time to celebrate. There is no time for an emotional outburst.

---

**player tip** - Consider where you want to be at the end of this practice, this game, or this season. Today is a step toward the best version of you. Progress is driven by where you've been — what came before. Progress is now, and it is ahead of you.

Remember how far you've come and enjoy the journey as you continue to build your skills. Every ball you see is a chance to improve your judgment, reflexes, and ability to catch it, field it, make the play. Have confidence in the hours spent mentally and physically preparing — your repetitions, your workouts, and your coaching.

**coach tip** - Encourage repeating the basics. Being fundamentally sound with proper mechanics will allow every athlete to be the best that they can be.

Allow for mistakes. Athletes must understand that mistakes are learning opportunities so they grow to believe in their training, abilities, and skills. Support the athlete even when the athlete performs less than optimally.

**parent tip** - Here are some suggestions for boosting self-esteem. It is key that your player has self-respect as an athlete and as a person. Also that the athlete has respect for their athletic skills and abilities. This is an internal reading measured by the athlete, not an external judgment made by a parent, coach, trainer, or teammate.

Athletes often wrongly determine self-worth by how successful they feel about their sport. They especially vulnerable to this problem because in sports, one is often judged by performance. If your athlete is a perfectionist, it can be further damaging to self-esteem because of high expectations and self-criticism of the player who is hard on themselves.

Guide your athlete to realize that athletic performance does not define who they are - it is just one dimension of what they do. An experience they have. An athlete's performance is just that — performance.

Don't make comparisons. Every player is a valuable asset to the team. Help your athlete understand the value that they bring.

## CROPS

Build your tool set, nurture success — in baseball and in life.

**Confidence**: look at how far you've come in building your understanding of baseball;

**Repetition**: study the game in different ways — watch it, read about it, play it;

**Optimism**: keep focused on the moment and what you can do to make the best of it;

**Process**: put your skills in play and enjoy making the best of the situation;

**Success**: think about what went right and do more of that.


*"Baseball is a game where a curve is an optical illusion,*
*a screwball can be a pitch or a person,*
*stealing is legal and you can spit anywhere you like*
*except in the umpire's eye or on the ball."*
*— Jim Murray*

"*A knuckleball is a curve ball that doesn't give a damn.*"
— *Jimmy Cannon*

"*I know I've got to just keep throwing the ball.*
*That's what I do best.*"
— *Dan Marino*

"*This is a very simple game. You throw the ball, you*
*catch the ball, you hit the ball. Sometimes you win,*
*sometimes you lose, sometimes it rains.*"
— *Bull Durham.*

# FOUR: THROWING THE BALL

Making quality throws on a consistent basis is the goal for every player.

Quickness is a vital part of good defensive play. It is important to build quick hands and feet, as well as develop consistent accurate throwing.

To get rid of the ball quickly, catch it with two hands. If a player catches it with one hand, it is difficult to get rid of it in time quickly. Shift your feet and step toward your target to increase accuracy.

*"Sometimes when my feet are slow,*
*my throw (to first base) isn't good.*
*But when I move my feet,*
*the throw is straight every time. "*
*— Edwin Encarnacion*

Accuracy comes from alignment. In baseball and in life. Move toward your goal. Focus on what you aim to achieve. Think of how you would like things to turn out and fill your vision with thoughts of success. Enjoy the process, have confidence, go the distance.

When throwing from 3B to 1B, stay in motion. See the ball into the mitt of your teammate on first base. Use all of your focus. Engage your entire body to make it happen.

Throwing hard requires the large muscles of the body, including the legs and back — not just the arm. Step forward, aligned and moving straight at the target. A step to the side often generates sideways momentum making throws curl so they are less accurate.

**player tip** - Step toward your target. This assists accuracy and velocity. In baseball, as in life, move in the direction of your goal.

**coach tip** - Repetition is one of the most basic learning techniques. To make it even more impactful, deliver training to your athletes in at least six different ways. Tell them. Show them. Provide a variety of drills to reinforce the behavior. Then chances are high that it'll stick.

Focus on the process to foster a growth mindset, create an athlete-centered environment, and reduce stress for players.

**parent tip** - Reaching repetition levels to enable mastery means that your athlete needs more time on task. This is something many resist just because learning is difficult.

Break down skills and make them portable, enabling your athlete to work at it in small doses, any time they have a few moments. This will ease frustration while building the skill, and it will build tolerance for frustration.

And, ensure adequate rest time for muscles to repair and recover.

## LIFE SKILLS: MOVE THROUGH THE OUTCOME

Stay out of the results. This simply means that you do your best and expect the best while accepting what happens — the result.

See the strides you've made in the past to give you confidence for the future. In hindsight, ask yourself, "What did I learn?" rather than beating yourself up for making a mistake. Don't repeat or dwell on errors — adjust, make any necessary amends, and move on as fast as possible.

Build on your skill set. Continue to improve. Put your maximum effort into the demand of the moment.

Now is a new experience. This minute is a fresh start. Today is another day. Don't carry mistakes from one moment to the next. Don't bring unsupportive energy into the moment with worry.

Do carry forward the lessons you have learned, and then do better.

*"I did then what I knew how to do;*
*now that I know better, I do better."*
*— Maya Angelou*

*"Don't let the fear of striking out hold you back."*
*— Babe Ruth*

*"You can't think and hit at the same time."*
*— Yogi Berra*

*"Don't forget to swing hard, in case you hit the ball."*
*— Woodie Held*

*"You can't hit what you can't see."*
*— Walter Johnson*

*"Hitting is 50% above the shoulders."*
*— Ted Williams*

*"Swing hard, in case they throw the ball*
*where you're swinging."*
*— Duke Snider*

# FIVE: HITTING THE BALL

When you are hitting, it is nine players against one in the big picture. And in the small picture, it is batter up against the catcher and pitcher.

Much of hitting success is about making adjustments to the pitcher. In all of life, it is about making adjustments. Success is never achieved in a straight line. Life doesn't always go according to plan — same with baseball.

So when conditions change, you must adapt. If you're waiting for the perfect fastball, you might receive only sliders. Regardless of what happens, you can successfully work it — make adjustments in the things you can control.

When hitting, trust your skills. Trust your hands. Relax. Don't always try to hit so hard. Again, trust your hands. Be confident in your ability. Believe in your training, believe in your abilities and skills, and believe in your experience to prepare you.

And, when you are tired, selectively expend energy at the plate. Minimize swings. Load better. That will help.

Just like in life, manage your energy to get the job done. In physics, energy is defined as the capacity to work. In humans, energy comes from four main areas: body, emotion, mind, and spirit. In each, energy can be expanded and renewed. Nutrition, exercise, sleep, and rest support basic energy levels of the body. The ability to manage emotions, being aware of how you feel and the impact on effectiveness — and the ability to move yourself into supportive feelings such as confidence will boost energy. Focus your attention to boost energy levels with mindfulness. And, charge your energy with the spirit of enjoying what you are doing, and doing it to the best of your ability.

## TIMING

Like many things in life, hitting is a lot about timing. Adapt, make adjustments, and time up your swing with the pitch. When you don't swing the bat, you lose timing. Your body forgets how to get the job done. Keep working your swing, even during the off-season.

*"A baseball swing is a very finely tuned instrument.*
*It is repetition, and more repetition,*
*then a little more after that."*
*— Reggie Jackson*

When you're standing at home plate and the pitch is coming down the line, you take a swing with the bat, you're in the game. You swing and you may miss. The second time you might get a piece of it and foul off the ball, the third time you ground out to 3B. Next time you get up to bat and you hit it into the outfield for a triple! By failing 70% of the time, you become a darn good hitter!

Put it out there. Figure out what works; and find out what doesn't work. Work on the basics. Fine-tune your mechanics. And continue to learn as you go.

## REPETITION

Repetition rules. As a skill is practiced over time, the activity becomes reflexive. The brain reinforces particular skills for balance and motion. An athlete repeats the same technique thousands of times in the same way to get it to stick.

Build muscle memory. When you repeat a movement over time, you create a long-term muscle memory for that task, eventually allowing it to be performed without conscious effort. Athletes and performers in a variety of fields develop muscle memory by practicing the same activities over and over again, with corrections of form as necessary. You want muscle memory to reflect the correct way to perform the skill. Your attitude is also important.

Practice with confidence. Let go of anxiety and allow your body to become comfortable with your swing.

*"Three or four times a game, a player has to execute a difficult task. He has to hit a very small ball, spinning at a very high speed, a very far distance."*

## MECHANICS

A hitter's stance or starting position can be just as important as swing mechanics. As always — in life, in baseball, and in hitting — it is important to work on the basics. Continue to fortify the foundation of your swing.

Again, it is important to develop muscle memory for the correct swing. Take your time and focus on the number of quality swings you take. Concentrate. Find the swing that works for you and repeat it every time you. Find your rhythm and you'll have your swing.

Like all athletics, hitting relies on core power moves. "Supine heel pushes will fortify your hamstring health, which is essential for sprinting," says Cindy Larson. To do these, simply lay on your back and drive your heels into the floor as you raise your hips to full extension creating a bridge between your shoulders and your feet. Hold. Release. Repeat.

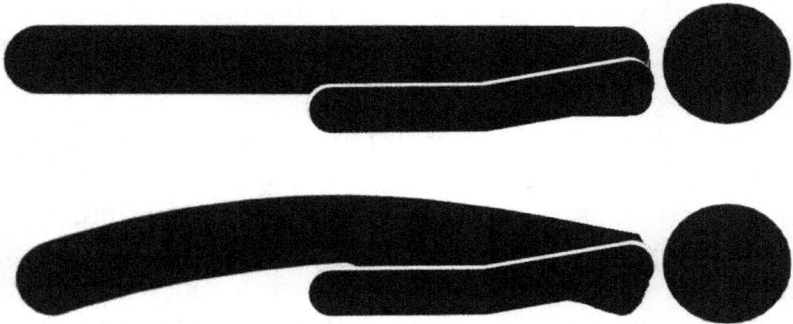

*"You obviously want the results*
*but you must do your job in every at-bat*
*and deal with what every situation dictates."*
*— Anthony Rizzo*

Make time to practice and to work on technical aspects; but not when you are at bats. When you get in the box, it is time to trust your work and get the job done. Focus on the pitch. Read it. Watch the spin. Follow through your bat when you choose to swing, or to the glove when it is a ball.

*"A full mind is an empty bat."*
*— Branch Rickey*

You practice to build trust and confidence. Don't break down the details of your swing while you're swinging. When you are up to bat, it is time to trust your skills and your instincts. Go do your job. Let your self-step up, show up, and do it.

## WALK

When you get to four balls before getting three strikes, take your base! It is called a walk. That's a win.

*"I'd rather have you walk*
*with the bases loaded."*
*— Earl Weaver*

## SWING

When the pitch looks good, time it up and SWING! Trust your instincts. Keep your eye on the ball all the way to the bat! You will definitely not get a hit if you don't swing.

## BUNT

Learn the art of bunting. Your coach will call for it when it is strategically needed. A bunt is a managed hit where the batter holds the bat in front of the plate, with hands extended on the ends of the bat, and taps the ball into play.

The goal is to get the ball to gently roll and force the infielders to scramble for it. Often this is called a sacrifice bunt where the batter gets out at first base but advances the runner(s) on base.

## STRIKE OUT

Don't let the fear of striking out keep you away from playing the game. Each strike in baseball is practice. It is the foundation for your hits, and for your home run.

*About whether he bats lefty or righty:*
*"Switch. I hit both home runs AND base hits."*
*— Domingo Ayala*

## EVALUATION

Of the "five tools" of baseball, three are traditionally considered batting tools in producing runs: Hitting, Power, and Speed. Add to this On Base and we get the HOPS method for evaluating the skills of baseball offense. In his book, Andre Lower outlines HOPS Baseball's four Batting Skills in detail. Here is a brief summary.

**Hitting:** This is the traditional batting average. Swing the bat. Make solid contact with the ball. Beat the fielders and get on base.

**On Base Average:** Measures walks and hit by pitch plus hits. Reflects ability to get on base. This is based predominantly on the batter's observation skills. Or the pitcher falling apart.

**Power:** This reflects the distance the ball is hit resulting in extra bases — doubles, triples, and home runs.

**Speed:** This is all about running, fast. Again, speed is its own skill and must be trained.

It is of interest since there are many facets to the baseball offense — batting is an intricate art.

## BATTING ORDER

Typically, the first three batters are the most consistent hitters — players who get on base. It's common for the leadoff hitter to be one of the fastest players on the team. Get a player on base in the first inning and have him steal a base right after can make the pitcher uncomfortable from the start.

The fourth batter is often called the 'clean-up hitter' and is positioned to bring home the baserunners. The end of the lineup is often seated with strategic players. Some coaches end the lineup with players who could be leadoff- hitters, balancing out the lineup so they can get on base. Then when the top of the lineup comes back around, there are "ducks on the pond" and they can bring them home to score.

*"Every hitter likes fastballs*
*just like everybody likes ice cream."*
*— Reggie Jackson*

## PRACTICE PRACTICE PRACTICE

Like with many things in life, when you don't swing the bat, your body forgets how you want to get the job done. Keep in the swing by practicing regularly — even if you only have time to imagine hitting the ball.

There's a time to work on the technical aspects of your swing — but not during your at-bats! When you are at the plate, trust your skills and your instincts. Do your job.

*"Well, boys, it's a round ball and a round bat*
*and you got to hit the ball square."*
*— Joe Schultz*

Remember, there are only four things that can happen when you are up to bat:

- The pitcher will mess with your mind and rattle you so you lose focus and efficiency.

- The pitcher will throw four balls and walk you (or the pitcher will hit you with a pitch and you will take your base).

- The pitcher will throw pitches that mess with your timing and your swing, and you will strike out.

- You will hit the ball... and put it in play.

You can manage your mind. You can control this one. Don't let the pitcher (or defense) mess with your head. Stay in control. Then, you have a good chance of winning the at-bat. Or you will make the pitcher work for the strike out.

Everything is neutral. You give it meaning. Nothing is anything until you make it something — and then it becomes what you make it. Everything just is, reality is personal. Get up to the plate. Do your best. Let go of the outcome.

*"This is the only game where you can fail 7 out of 10 times and be considered an All-Star."*
*— Danny Patterson*

**player tip** - Swing your bat on plane with the baseball, advises Drew Beuerlein. A pitcher is taught to throw downhill. If you chop the ball, you have no chance of meeting it square. If the plane of your swing matches the plane of the pitch, you have a great chance for success.

**coach tip** - Look for the possibilities for every player. A fast runner might be perceived to be a poor hitter. Perhaps teaching this player to bunt or to switch hit will allow the team to take advantage of speed and base running.

To assist pitch recognition in batting practice, consider using a shortened "ghost bat" so hitters can face pitchers, call out the pitch, swing, and get their timing without concern for fielding the ball.

**parent tip** - Support your player in developing a feel for hitting. This means regular swinging. Work with your athlete when you can and consider getting a tee and a net (or other batting tools) for when you are not available.

*"Guessing what the pitcher is going to throw is eighty percent of being a successful hitter; the other twenty percent is just execution."*
— *Hank Aaron*

## KNOW THE PITCH

When you are up to bat, look for clues to identify the pitch. The faster you identify a pitch, the easier it is to hit. Learn to recognize pitch types.

See the ball right out of the pitcher's hand. Read the pitch — fastball, change-up, or breaking ball, and then making the swing adjustment — so you are not fooled by it. Focus on the pitcher's release point and pick up cues.

Here is a list of twelve common pitches and their tendencies:

### Fastballs:

**Four-seam** — The fastest, straightest pitch, it has little to no movement.

**Two-seam** (or Sinker) — Moves downward, and depending on release, will sometimes run in on the right corner of the plate.

**Cutter** — Faster than a slider with more movement than a fastball, this pitch tends to cut to the left at the plate.

**Splitter** — Breaks down suddenly before reaching plate.

**Forkball** — Breaks like a splitter, but more gradual, less sudden downward movement.

### Breaking Balls:

**Curveball** — Top to bottom movement, often called 12-6, like clock hands at 12 and 6. 121

**Slider** — Mix of a fastball and a curve, a slider breaks down and left at the plate.

**Slurve** — Like a curve with lateral movement to the left.

**Screwball** — The slurve that has lateral moment to the right.

## Changeups:

**Changeup** — Thrown with the same arm motion as fastball, but slower, off-speed.

**Palmball** — Even slower than a changeup, the ball is gripped tightly in palm and thrown with the same arm motion as a fastball.

**Circle Changeup** — Acts like a faster screwball.

Things to watch for to help you identify a pitch:

- **Rotation** - notice how the ball is spinning
- **Movement** - the general direction the ball is moving
- **Break** - a sudden shift in direction
- **Release** - where does the pitcher let go of the ball
- **Grip** - how is the pitcher holding the ball

*"Life will always throw you curves,*
*just keep fouling them off;*
*the right pitch will come, and when it does,*
*be prepared to run the bases."*
*— Rick Maksian*

# SIX: BASE RUNNING

An athlete with speed has huge advantages in any sport, including baseball. One of the keys to winning a baseball game is the ability to take extra bases. When you are at bat, base running begins once you put the bat on the baseball, or once you get a walk or are hit by a pitch and get on first base. When there are players on base, it is often referred to as "ducks on the pond."

*"I can still steal a base anytime I get ready."*
*— Rickey Henderson*

## BASE RUNNING

Base running is the act of running around the bases and is performed by members of the team on offense. It is a tactical part of the game with the goal of reaching home to score a run. Batting produces base runners and helps move base runners along, all the way home. It is interesting that first, second and third bases are square bags while home plate actually looks like home. Upside down home, that is.

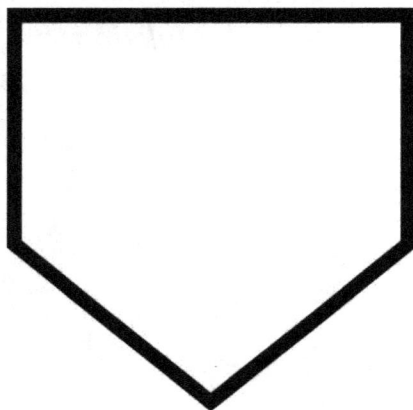

When the ball is hit, you become a runner. Get in the habit of running it out to first base every time the bat hits the ball. The coach will signal whether to run through the base or whether to turn toward second base. Look ahead. Focus on where you are going. Commit to the path and you can make adjustments as needed.

An important factor in base running is putting pressure on the defense, creating mistakes that can turn into runs for your team. Once you're on first base, take a lead, disrupt the pitcher's timing, and get to second base.

Run out every ball. A grounder isn't an automatic out. A player hustling down the line puts pressure on the fielder who has to act quickly to throw out the runner — so chances of making a mistake increase. Stress on the play makes defense work faster. That's when errors happen.

When practicing base running and conditioning, ingrain habits that help take advantage of situations that arise during games. Be in a position to make the most of an opportunity — like taking a single and stretching it into a double.

*"You can't score runs if you can't run the bases."*
*— Unknown*

To be a good base runner, be aware of the play around you. Think two bases ahead and consider 'how am I going to accomplish getting there?' Hard work, desire, and hustle will get you there. To do it, maximize speed with minimal strides. Know where you are going and be ready to go the distance.

**SLIDING**

The most useful, safest slide is the pop-up slide. Go feet first. Use your momentum when you hit the bag to pop up quickly and continue running if needed. Extend one leg, place the ankle of your other leg under the hamstring of your straight leg. Keep both your hands up (a good time to have on your batting gloves) so when you make contact with the ground you will not slam your wrists. Make contact with the ground with your bent knee and the upper part of the back of your straight leg.

Head first or belly slide has a high risk of injury. It may get you into the base a little quicker than going feet first because you keep your forward momentum. But, exercise caution when employing this slide. Some teams advise against sliding headfirst and for only sliding feet first.

---

**GREAT PLAY** *The runner rounded third and raced to beat the throw to home. As he approached the plate and prepared to slide, the catcher scoops the ball and squats to lean in for the tag. Instead of sliding, the runner leaps over the catcher, landing on home plate as the astonished umpire motions with sweeping arms, "SAFE!" A great example of quick thinking, determination, and instinct.*

---

## STEALING

Stealing second base is the most common and effective way for fast base runners to take extra bases. Learn not to make the first or third out at 3rd base. Know your speed and understand when to take a chance versus when to play it more conservative.

*"I'm convinced that every boy, in his heart, would rather steal second base than an automobile."*
*— Tom Clark*

Develop your instincts... One key to good base running is to recognize the signals from your opposing pitcher. Did the pitcher's head go down?

Then the pitch is to the plate. Is the pitcher's head coming up? The throw is coming to first base for the pickoff.

*PRO PROFILE: Rickey Henderson, Hall of Fame outfielder, played 25 seasons in the majors. He led the league in steals 12 times, seven consecutively. His career total stolen bases of 1,406 is the most ever in baseball. His 2,295 runs is also the highest in MLB history.*

## THE PICKLE

A pickle, also known as a rundown, happens when a baserunner is stranded between two bases. The runner attempts to get to the next base (not on a force) and is cut off by the defensive player who has the live ball. The runner turns around, attempting to return to the previous base before being tagged out.

Meanwhile, the defense player throws the ball past the base runner to the previous base player, forcing the runner to reverse directions again. This back and forth is repeated until the runner is put out or safely reaches a base.

The runner must get by the fielder who is without the ball while there is no other fielder to cover the base. The pickle drill is great for training both base running and fielding — especially accurate throwing.

There are many fine points of base running to master. Practice and technique building in this ability will add another element of skill and prowess to your game.

**player tip** - Always run hard through home, especially with two outs. If a runner gets thrown out trying to stretch a single into a double and you touch home before the out happens, your run counts.

**coach tip** - Instruct players to hit and run. Once they feel the bat on the ball, make that a trigger to head for first base. Train them to look at the first base coach and follow the signal — run through the base, round it, stop for a foul ball. Then, when this habit is instilled, teach runners to take a peek of the field after taking a couple steps toward the base to give them awareness of the play.

**parent tip** - Find ways to run with your athlete. Play tag, tennis, or volleyball. Speed is important. And so is agility.

Agility is one of the primary movement skills needed for successful participation in multidirectional sports. It is important training for reducing risk for injury. Agility is the ability to maintain posture stability in conditions requiring changes in speed and direction in response to demand.

Everything in exercise is a progression or a regression. Make sure your athlete has a balance of workout activity: Flexibility. Speed. Agility. Quickness. Core — a strong core is always critical to performance. Rest to repair and reset.

*"If you are persistent you will get it.
If you're consistent, you will keep it."*
*— Unknown*

*"You just can't beat the person who never gives up."*
*— Babe Ruth*

*"The harder you WORK the LUCKIER you get!"*
*— Gary Player*

*"There are really only two conditions
of the human experience:
very, very happy
or about to become very, very happy."*
*— Unknown*

# SEVEN: TALENT, SKILL, HARD WORK

There are only two things you can control: your ATTITUDE and your EFFORT. it takes zero talent to outwork someone. And, since baseball is a game of failure, how you handle failure determines your success. Build that talent.

With the right attitude, you can easily turn every difficulty into an opportunity and every obstacle into an occasion for growth.

*"Good luck doesn't exist; you predict your luck*
*with the hard work you put in."*
*— Jorge Minyety*

## HARD WORK, SKILL & TALENT

It is said that: Hard work beats talent when talent doesn't work. In other words, it takes zero talent to outwork someone. But, don't let these words mess with you. Success is about gaining experience, practicing, and achieving mastery of a skill.

*"Talent is 90 percent made, not born."*
*— Malcolm Gladwell*

You are told you have talent. Interpret that as: "My skills are so much better than before!" Give credit to your commitment and to your practice. The time and energy you have given to working on drills and playing the game, that is what has built your skill set and allowed your talent to thrive. Talent is up to you. Pick where you want to excel and get to work.

*"Do you want to know who you are? Don't ask.*
*Act! Action will delineate and define you."*
*— Thomas Jefferson*

**player tip** - Having talent is having a flair or knack for something... you may have a natural strength in an area that supports your ability in your sport, and your practice will develop that talent into a skill. Keep up the good work and you will continue to grow your skill set and your talent. Use it or lose it.

**coach tip** - Instead of telling a player "you have talent," tell them that you see their work paying off. This way, they feel a sense of accomplishment. And the message is that they have control of their developing skill set.

**parent tip** - Remind your athlete that doing the work will result in improved skills. Shift away from results-oriented thinking to focus on the process. Focus on the process will lead to mastery, growth, and performance.

*"The best possible thing in baseball
is winning the World Series.
The second best thing is
losing the World Series."*
— *Tommy Lasorda*

*"In baseball, there's always the next day."*
— *Ryne Sandberg*

*"Don't get too high when things are going well,
and don't get too low one things are tough."*
— *Drew Beuerlein*

# EIGHT: WINNING & LOSING

As we grow up, it is important to believe that we can, and will, do great things. The feeling of winning, the need to feel a sense of dominance, to display skill to feel strong in relation to others, helps boost self-esteem.

Winning and bragging can offer temporary relief from feelings of failure. How can we learn to accept defeat gracefully? The ability to accept defeat gracefully is learned through practice and the emulation of admired adults. Learn from competition the importance of teamwork and cooperation, commitment to others, and respect for opponents.

*"It is difficult to bring people to goodness with lessons, but it is easy to do so by example."*
*— Seneca*

Life, like baseball teaches that the one who wins is likely the team that "thinks" the most moves ahead. And, sometimes, even that is not enough. Stop looking at it as surrendering or losing to the other side. Instead, focus on where you are growing.

In the course of a game, there will always be moments of excitement, anxiety, frustration, disappointment. Play with enthusiasm and express excitement and disappointment, in appropriate ways. Stay in the moment and you will have the best possible result.

Winning or losing is a team result. Each player contributes to the outcome — whether handling the ball or encouraging the play. Play hard. Give it your best in every moment. Support one another. Then move to the next play.

## SPORTSMANSHIP

It is always fun to win. And, someone has to lose every time. Sometimes, that will be your team. Respect your opponent. Build your capacity for sportsmanship, foster your self-esteem, and choose your role models. Be a gracious winner. Be a respectful loser.

*"I never thought of losing, but now that it's happened, the only thing is to do it right; we all have to take defeats in life."*
*— Muhammad Ali*

Losing is not as fun as winning. It can be frustrating, disappointing, and discouraging. If your self-worth is tied up with the outcome of a competition, then losing can be threatening to your sense of self. Recognize feelings of insecurity. Learn to appropriately handle this sometimes unpleasant, very common, and valuable life experience. It is all about how you choose to show up. how you respond.

---

*ABOUT PERSPECTIVE They are tied. One out. Overtime. Bases loaded. All of the players are 12 years old. He is 12 years old. The closer. Parents of the AT-bat team holler "Kill him!" Strike! Strike! Foul! Foul! "Kill him!" Ball. Foul! Strike! Two out. Next batter. Coach pulls the defense to the infield. Strike! "Kill him!" Ball. The umpire warns the parents to behave. Strike! "Kill him!" they continue. Foul. Foul. Ball in play.*

*A weak fly ball lands just where the Shortstop would usually stand. Run scores. Game over.*

*Despite poor sportsmanship of parents and fans, the opposition takes the championship. Loss of role modeling.*

*When asked how he handled the verbal threats, the closer replied, "I pretended that they were cheering for me." Winning attitude.*

Winning can be exhilarating. And, again, it is key to manage the surge of emotion. Show good sportsmanship.

*"I hit a home run I had a habit of running*
*the bases with my head down;*
*I figured the pitcher already felt bad enough*
*without me showing him up rounding the bases."*
*— Mickey Mantle*

We all experience a wide range of emotions internally. How you deal with your emotions determines your character. Honor your opponent. Meet with victory and defeat. Find the joy in having done your best. Let a loss fuel your determination to get the next one. Results will change.

Look at your return on effort. What did you do that worked? What can you do to improve for next time? Your perceived weakness could be a powerful strength.

*"The efforts you make will surely be rewarded.*
*If not, then you are simply not ready*
*to call them efforts."*
*— Sadaharu Oh*

Remain consistent. Get out of emotional highs and lows, and maintain a steady arch of satisfaction, momentum and growth. Former pro catcher Drew Beuerlein shares this advice he received from his father:

*"Never let anyone know if you are 3 for 3, or 0 for 3;*
*don't ride the emotional roller coaster."*
*— Mr. Beuerlein*

Meet every challenge as it arises. You are asked for nothing more than to give it your best every time you are at bat or in the field. And that is everything you can ask of yourself, also.

*"Always make a total effort, even when the odds are against you."*
*— Arnold Palmer*

**EFFORT** [noun] *a vigorous or determined attempt.*

Todd Herman of The Peak Athlete helps players get out of their own way and to achieve their full potential. He provides this acronym for EFFORT.

**Execution.** Do your best. Consistently build on your skill set. This doesn't mean perfect; it means the best of your improving ability. Focus. Keep your mind in the game.

**Focus** on the process not the end results.

**Feedback.** Get consistent evaluation loops via comments, assessments, reactions, observation, results, and follow-up.

**Optimization.** Set strategies to employ your skill set and give you the best.

**Routine.** Create habits that support your success.

**Toughness.** Be resilient. Look for the lesson and realize opportunity in every moment.

So, what are some tools you can employ to boost your effort and effectiveness? Crush stress by building confidence. Thwart distractions by fortifying focus. End negative thinking with positive habits and supportive self- talk. Strategize to prevent pitfalls of poor game planning. Focus on the process.

## FOCUS ON THE PROCESS

Process is performance, right here, right now — this step. Be focused and in the moment. Block distractions. Recognize that the outcome is feedback. Based on the result, adjust or carry on to realize the optimal outcome. Remember, you are the effort, never the outcome. Remain in the moment, focused on the process of each individual play. Rely on your training, skills, and abilities.

*"Never confuse a single defeat with a final defeat."*
*— F. Scott Fitzgerald*

Sportsmanship is important for players, coaches, parents, and fans. Competitive sport can be an emotional roller coaster. The experience frequently pulls a variety of emotions from deep within us. As an athlete, parent and coach, it's critical to handle intense emotions that get stimulated by tough losses and failures, and to remain gracious when winning.

**player tip** - Know and believe that you have done everything possible to prepare. This gives you a mental edge over the competition and increases belief in your skills and abilities. Knowledge and belief in your skills allows you to step up and freely apply your abilities during competition.

Don't hold back. Do your best, and then — win or lose — be ready to move on to the next opportunity. Always look for ways to become a better version of yourself. You are the effort, not the outcome.

**coach tip** - Emphasize the importance of teamwork and cooperation, commitment to others, and respect for opponents. Encourage players to look at the results as feedback for what worked and for what didn't — what else might be more effective; recognize the skill of the other team; then let go of the outcome and get on to the next play — or the next game.

**parent tip** - Ask your player to evaluate their effort and results. Then congratulate what worked and reinforce the opportunities to improve.

Lead by example and appropriately express excitement or disappointment. Don't be tied up in the outcome of your athlete's performances. Focus on the effort. Win or lose, it's about how they play the game, and how they show up in life.

*"If things go wrong,*
*don't go with them."*
*— Roger Babson*

*"A setback ain't nothin' but an opportunity
for a comeback."*
*— Harold Craig Reynolds*

*"Once you can accept failure,
you can have fun and success."*
*— Rickey Henderson*

*"If you have a bad day in baseball,
and start thinking about it,
you will have 10 more."*
*— Sammy Sosa*

*"Life is 10% what happens to you
and 90% how you react to it."*
*— Charles R Swindoll*

*"It never ceases to amaze me
how many of baseball's wounds are self-inflicted."*
*— Bill Veeck*

# NINE: THE MENTAL GAME

So much of what happens to us in life, and on the baseball field, is about what we think. If you yourself can't believe that you can hit the ball or field it, then who will? Remember the line from *The Little Engine That Could*: "I think I can." Repeat it and make it your signature phrase.

*"If you even dream of beating me,*
*you'd better wake up and apologize."*
*— Muhammad Ali*
*(Cassius Marcellus Clay, Jr)*

## THE MENTAL GAME

Mental toughness is about meeting moment-to-moment battles with courage and commitment to yourself and to the experience. In life, in every endeavor, there are three battles that you will encounter.

**The first battle is inside you.** This fight is about fortifying your commitment to do your best, not succumbing to mediocrity. It is about steeling your resolve and being persistent, maintaining an offensive mindset. It's about overcoming obstacles such as fear by developing skills, knowledge and personal power. This is the most crucial battle to win — and it is the one you have the power to win, every time. So tell yourself "I think I can" and then go out and do it!

**The second battle is between you and the environment.** The environment is everything around you. It includes everything from nature and weather, to culture, expectations, and protocol. Show up on time. Be respectful and responsible. Honor the rules. Take the heat. Stay focused and determined. Accept the results. Let go of the outcome. Carry on.

In baseball, it's about sportsmanship. The system can be downright cruel sometimes. A bad call by the ump. The coach telling you to "go" and the opponent throws you out with an amazing, unexpected effort!

And the elements can work for or against you. The wind takes the ball off path of your judgment. Your primary power is how you respond — with respectfulness. You win this battle by accepting results and adhering to the rules.

*"There was a perception of me, and I earned it*
*because I was really intense, really gruff.*
*I treated certain people poorly at times.*
*It was because of who I was.*
*It was almost my strength. I came in all business.*
*I tried to find ways to fit in with that demeanor,*
*but it's not easy."*
*— Kirk Gibson*

**The third battle is the actual engagement.** In baseball, it's the game. The umpire shouts, "Play Ball," and the battle begins. A game is often the easiest of the fights, and often the shortest in time invested. In this effort, you show up with intention and focus. You bring your best effort to every challenge. Whether fielding, hitting, or cheering on your team, you are all in it! You win some, you lose some — that is the outcome. Let go of the outcome. You are the effort. The prizes will be there.

Focus on that first battle — the fight in your mind. Remember, that is the one you can win every time. Win that before you ever embark on the second battle — the system — or have to deal with the consequences of the third — a game — and you will be in the best position to win all three, every time.

105

Win the fight in your mind before stepping foot onto the baseball field, into the classroom, toward your dream. This is true for any situation in life. So then, the question is: How?

Here are some of the many mental toughness tactics you can use in managing your mind before you step onto the baseball field or into the battles of life. These have been employed by many people in many fields — military, sports, medicine, business. Find what is comfortable and do what works for you.

**Breath Control:** Simply focus on your breath to reduce stress in any situation. Improve your breathing to better serve your body. Breath from the diaphragm — imagine your stomach as a balloon filling with air then releasing it.

**Positive Self-Talk**: Positive self-talk can detach us from negative thoughts and help goad us into pushing further. A mantra or a short, simple phrase, repeated actively will prevent negative and disempowering thoughts.

**Visualization:** Vividly imagine a desired scenario — focusing on the process, not just the outcome — include overcoming obstacles that are likely to pop up along the way. Engage as many senses as possible: sight, hearing, smell, touch, taste, feelings, etc.

**Micro Goals:** Focus your mind on one thing — the next action. When the overall task seems daunting, one-step at a time is completely doable.

Set your mind on your goal. Results often reflect what you THINK will happen. Develop your inner power of positive thinking, persistence, and confidence. Never think of failing.

*"Whether you think that you can,*
*or that you can't,*
*you are usually right."*
*— Henry Ford*

Do your homework before every game. Increase your awareness of what may happen. Then in the game, focus. Block out distraction. Stop any concern about who's watching and what they might be thinking.

Accept the idea of a failure as part of the journey to your goals. The thing about goals is that when you fail to meet them, there is usually an opportunity to re-assess, adjust if needed, and re-commit, after stumbling.

*"Show me a guy who's afraid to look bad,*
*and I'll show you a guy you can beat every time."*
*— Lou Brock*

It is said again and again; baseball is a game of failure. You win it by reducing the failures and by making the most out of every situation. When you make a mistake, how you think about the mistake matters more than the mistake itself.

Whether you're afraid, or averse, or uncomfortable with mistakes, the result is the same — you hold back. Worrying about mistakes gives them power over you. You cause our own suffering. Remember, when you make mistakes, you grow.

You are stronger today than you were yesterday. Though you might be encountering the same or a similar problem, this time it's with a different view and an enriched perspective. You are acting from a more experienced place today.

Failure is not learning from your mistakes. Learn from them and failure becomes a lesson, an exercise, an exercise that teaches you.

*"If you learn from your mistakes in baseball, it can*
*teach you a lot about life."*
*— Drew Beuerlein*

107

## BUILD CONFIDENCE

Confidence comes from recognizing that the decisions you make are correct. Learn the game. Be vocal. Make your decisions with confidence. Know the reasons for decisions your coaches make.

Fortify confidence with training. Remind yourself of all you have done to be prepared — and trust that work! Don't compare yourself to others, play your best game. Focus on things you can control.

While you can't control your opponent, the officials, weather, field conditions, the past, the outcome, other peoples' expectations, you are in charge of how you respond and react to everything. Focus on being responsive.

Realize that everyone makes mistakes. Face up to those mistakes and learn from them. Take charge of the situation by owning it. Find the upside and coach yourself — learn from it, forgive it, let go, go on.

*"The principle is competing against yourself — it's about self-improvement, about being better than you were the day before."*
*— Steve Young*

Don't let anyone tell you you're too short, too small, to weak — can't throw hard enough or can't hit the ball far enough. Everybody has an opinion. Don't let others define you. Have commitment to your game and go after it with confidence. Bring your strengths to the field and play ball! Let your love of the game guide you.

*"Do not let anybody dictate what you want — follow your dreams."*
*— Jorge Minyety*

Take the chance. Never let anyone tell you that you cannot do what you dream to do.

---

**JORGE'S STORY** *When I was working really hard to get drafted I had a few coaches and scouts that didn't believe in me. One time, my dad called my coach to ask how I was doing and the coach said I wasn't good enough to play Pro. My dad didn't mention anything to me at the time — so important and so smart. Another scout told my dad I was too small. Again, my dad didn't say anything. I continued putting all my effort into what I love so much — baseball. After the years went by, I got drafted by the San Diego Padres. My dad was really proud of me. Then, he told me about all the people that didn't believe in me. He mentioned them, one by one... And I could see his pride.*

*Still, in my heart, I was like OH MY GOD... Because if he had told me then what these people had said about me, I might have gotten discouraged. Who knows, maybe I would have quit playing baseball, or I would have lost motivation. My dad never said anything. He let me work hard after my dream.*

*The San Diego Padres opened a new baseball complex — a 10-million-dollar facility for us. All the news people were there, plus all the people that my dad mentioned. It felt really good that they saw me there in my professional uniform. — Jorge Minyety*

---

Let your mistakes be your motivation, not your excuse. Use them as stepping-stones. Mistakes teach important lessons. Every time you make a mistake, you're one-step closer to your goal.

In baseball, and in life, dwell on the positive. Stop beating up yourself and instead realize you are stronger for the experience. The worst thing you can do is obsess over a mistake. The more you focus on something, the more significance it begins to have. Refocus. Move on.

So, if you don't like something, change it. If you can't change it, change the way you think about it. Getting frustrated takes you off balance. It is a vicious spiral. Negative thinking creates more negativity and ends up in negative results. Positive thinking always leads to the most positive results.

Another tool is to be aware of what you feel versus your emotions. Learn from emotions and respond appropriately to them.

**ANGER:** My rights have been violated.

**ANXIETY:** Something bad is going to happen.

**EMBARRASSMENT:** I've lost standing in someone's eyes.

**FEAR:** I don't have all the information about this.

**FRUSTRATION:** I don't have the resources I require.

**GUILT:** I've violated someone else's rights.

**SADNESS:** I've lost something.

**SHAME:** I've broken my own standards.

When you understand your emotions, you can own them. Then you can respond to them with appropriate action. There is always a solution.

*"I learned you have to control your emotions and learn to use them, not let them use you."*
*— Trent Clark"*

Errors can cost you; mental errors can keep you out of the game. Baseball is a game of failure. How you handle failure determines your success. One basic principle to apply in difficulty is this — never quit. To give up is complete defeat. If you really want to fix any mistake, then your best bet is to learn more about the game and to practice your skills.

*"A perfectionist expects to be perfect;*
*if you're not perfect,*
*you're frustrated, and it leads*
*you into a negative cycle."*
*— Max Scherzer*

Accept that you will never reach perfection and that every play you make is the best you could do at that time. Look for a new opportunity in each moment. Be tougher than the tough situation. Don't quit. Don't get emotional. You'll always get an idea or see an opportunity if you don't panic.

*"You have power over your mind, not outside events;*
*realize this, and you will find strength."*
*— Marcus Aurelius*

In baseball, as in life, there are only two things you can control: your ATTITUDE and your EFFORT. Be ready. Prepare physically and mentally to give it your all. Trust your skills. Rely on your instincts. Step toward your target. Believe in your training, believe in your abilities and skills, and believe in your past experiences to prepare for and perform well in a game or event. Just like in life.

*"I never think about having a bad game*
*because I have prepared."*
*— David Robinson*

Win it! Each moment, each play, each pitch, each at bat, etc. is a chance to win in the moment. Do your best. Adjust as required. Do your best again.

That's baseball. That's life.

## DON'T GIVE UP

Recognize some of the unproductive self-protective games your mind is playing — and stop playing them! They all amount to giving up on yourself.

Quitting before you even start might seem to protect you from losing — if you don't enter the game (that's any aspect of life you're avoiding), you can't lose. Well, you can't win either.

*"There is no failure except in no longer trying."*
*— Chris Bradford*

Or, if you quit mid-stream, before the game is over, you might be a quitter, but you've saved yourself from being a loser. But your loss is actually bigger. You lost the whole experience. Win or lose, you learn and grow by doing. If your thought is negative, "what could go wrong?" change it to support you, "what must I do to optimize outcome?"

*"Failure should be our teacher, not our undertaker.*
*Failure is delay, not defeat. It is a temporary detour,*
*not a dead end. Failure is something*
*we can avoid only by saying nothing,*
*doing nothing, and being nothing."*
*— Denis Waitley*

If you think or say, "I didn't care anyway," you never committed to yourself, your team, or the game, so it doesn't matter that you lost. This is another way to give up.

*"Giving up is the only sure way to fail."*
*— Gena Showalter*

If you decide that the game's stupid, and it doesn't matter that you lost, you are only hurting yourself. There is no dumb game. Every event is a chance to show up and do something. Make the experience count.

*"Only those who dare to fail greatly
can ever achieve greatly."
— Robert F. Kennedy*

If you keep halfheartedly playing the game without ever coming to a place where you win or lose, it becomes an endless game. Then at least you haven't lost. And you can never win. Play to get the best outcome. Play to win the moment.

*"Success is stumbling from failure to failure
with no loss of enthusiasm."
— Winston Churchill*

**player tip** - Think your way to success. Consider 'I can be successful because'...

• I control my actions.

• I get better and better each day.

• Nobody can take away my effort.

• I can tap into a mountain of information.

• I'm coachable and willing to learn from others.

Believing in yourself and trusting the work you do will go a long way, in baseball and in life.

Establish a routine that will prepare you for the game. By using physical actions to get physically and mentally ready for play, you will be focused and ready for the field.

> *"Ever tried. Ever failed. No matter.*
> *Try again. Fail again. Fail better."*
> *— Samuel Beckett*

**coach tip** - Give your players tips for regrouping when things get stressful. Controlling your breathing is helpful when dealing with tough situations, anxiety, or frustration. A simple breath exercise used by the U.S. Army and by Navy SEALS to manage stress is 4x4 breathing:

- Breathe in through your nose to the count of 4.
- Hold your breath to the count of 4.
- Breathe out through your mouth to the count of 4.
- Hold empty breath to the count of 4.
- Repeat until you feel your body and mind relax.

Remind players that they can use tactical breathing to help prepare for a game or to be ready for a stressful situation. It helps while actively dealing with stress. And, afterwards, tactical breathing assists a player to return to a more relaxed state.

> *"Growth is a spiral process, doubling back on itself,*
> *reassessing and regrouping."*
> *— Julia Margaret Cameron*

**parent tip** - Physical and mental errors are completely different types of errors and should be treated completely different. Find the "buttons to push" after physical or mental errors to motivate your player.

A physical error like dropping a fly ball, bobbling a grounder, or making a bad throw can be discouraging. After a physical error, comfort your player by saying something like "You'll get it next time!"

A mental error like throwing to the wrong base — even after you called outage play, or missing signals, or not hustling calls for a discussion. A common, appropriate response to a mental error is "Keep your head in the game. "When the player is interested in talking about the game, engage them in the process by inquiring "What happened?" Let them learn from looking at it objectively.

## LIFE TIP: ACCOUNTABILITY

Own your experience. When you make a mistake, own it. Step up and take responsibility. It will restore people's confidence — and your own — and it will increase your influence. Once you accept accountability and responsibility, suddenly everything is inside of your control. You can make a difference.

It is important to know to whom you are accountable. Yourself, your coach, your team.

Don't wallow in self-pity. Don't drown yourself in remorse. Take actions to correct problems you create. You can do that when you own it. Hone your skills. Shore up weaknesses. Lean on your strengths.

Use *I* sentences. Own your results. Be specific about your choices and the outcomes or results of them.

For instance: "I was surprised by the bounce the grounder took and I didn't respond quickly enough to field it" rather than "the grounder took a bad bounce."

This gives you the perspective that you can improve your reaction time rather than that you were a victim of circumstance. It puts the situation in your control.

## CROPS

Here is another chance to pull the weeds and plant the seeds of supportive habits.

**Confidence**: the first rule of building confidence is to do what needs to be done — action drives feelings of confidence; act confidently, then feel confident — don't wait to feel confident, go meet it head on;

**Repetition**: cycling information, repeating it in different ways over time, reinforces your understanding;

**Optimism**: there is always a best possible result — even if that means losing by fewer runs — find it;

**Process**: have a clear sense of the goals you desire achieving and then do the things required to accomplish them;

**Success**: never say I can't — say either "I won't" or "I will" to every challenge — take back your power.

*"Baseball is the only field of endeavor
where a man can succeed three times out of ten
and be considered a good performer."*
*— Ted Williams*

*"Once you can accept failure,
you can have fun and success."*
*— Rickey Henderson*

*"If you're going to play at all, you're out to win."*
*— Derek Jeter*

*"Every day is a new opportunity.
You can build on yesterday's success or put its failures
behind and start over again.
That's the way life is, with a new game every day,
and that's the way baseball is."*
*— Bob Feller*

# TEN: FAILURE

There are many ways to look at facets of life and experiences in the game of baseball. Failure is an aspect of winning and losing, and it is its own concept.

It's not a problem to make mistakes. However, it is a problem if you never learn from them. If you're afraid of failure, you won't attempt what needs to be done to achieve success. The solution is to make friends with failure. See it as the opportunity it is to learn and grow.

It is said that the difference between a master and a beginner is that the master has failed more times than the beginner has even tried. Sometimes things have to go wrong before success appears. Success is simply an accomplishment of a specific intention or goal.

*"You build on failure. You use it as a stepping stone.*
*Close the door on the past.*
*You don't try to forget the mistakes,*
*but you don't dwell on it.*
*You don't let it have any of your energy,*
*or any of your time, or any of your space."*
*— Johnny Cash*

Failure is personal. And it is guaranteed. You will fail. Often. No matter how much you prepare, becoming physically stronger and mentally smarter, there is no way to guarantee an absence of failure. You will absolutely, positively fail from time to time. The truth is that failures are part of success. There can be no success without failure.

*It's not about that you did something wrong*
*but that you realize what happened and change.*

Baseball is a game of failure. A batter who hits the ball and gets on base three times out of ten is a superstar. That is 30 percent success rate — which, in school, is a fail! Imagine coming home with 30 percent and a grade of an F on your test.

*"It's not the failures that define us*
*so much as how we respond."*
*— Shane Parrish*

In baseball, errors are a key part of the game. They are tracked and kept in a record for each player and for each team.

Remember: the PLAY, not the PLAYER, is under the microscope. Learn from success and from mistakes. The key is to recover from failures and setbacks, learn from them, go on to experience the success you desire and deserve.

*"Things could be worse;*
*imagine if your errors were counted*
*and published every day,*
*like those of a baseball player."*
*— Unknown*

Thinking on your feet is as important as knowing the game well. This is especially true in baseball. There are infinite possibilities of how a play will unfold. So have a strategy in mind and be ready to adjust as the play is set in motion. Watch for the opportunities as they arise. Be ready to capitalize on them.

Remember. Failure becomes a lesson when you learn from it. See it as feedback. Failure teaches that breaking down means a chance to build back up — it is a challenge, not an ending.

In baseball and in life, you cannot succeed unless you are willing to fail. Failure means you are attempting to do great things — working to get better and better in every way.

*"I tried to make the play too fast.*
*That's what I have to learn.*
*Stay aggressive, but try to do the routine.*
*Don't try to do too much."*
*— Edwin Encarnacion*

## MEET IT AND BEAT IT

Jack Canfield gives us this equation for success.

$$E+R=O$$

Events plus Response equals Outcome.

An event is anything that happens. You cannot always control what happens. It might rain. When it rains, the game might be played, delayed or canceled.

Your response to events is totally under your control. If it is raining and the game goes on, you could respond with enthusiasm because there is another challenge to meet — playing in the rain. Or you could let it "dampen your spirits" and then your response will reduce your enjoyment and possibly your success.

The outcome is the experience you have with the event based on your response to it. See things in a way that serves you.

Be responsible for yourself. Choose your response. Meet the event with your response and you will beat it by getting the optimal, or best possible outcome. Remember, blaming and complaining gives away your power. Own your experience. Here are some tools to assist you in meeting failure, or setbacks, with resilience.

*"Success is a few simple disciplines,*
*practiced every day;*
*while failure is simply a few errors in judgment,*
*repeated every day."*
*— Jim Rohn*

## MAKE FEAR YOUR FRIEND

Face your fear and rename it as excitement. Let fear fuel you to act more boldly. Channel it to boost your awareness. Take advantage of the energy surge fear can bring you and let it charge you to push through.

## HAVE POSITIVE SELF TALK

Take a look at your thoughts. Imagine what your life would be if you consistently told yourself good things. The next time you think about complaining, choose better words — choose to speak of the outcomes you desire. Focus on what you want. Then you get more of that.

*"I can do this."*

*"I have laser sharp focus."*

*"Okay, we will get the next one."*

Change your unproductive thoughts. Think of a thought you have that disempowers you and ask yourself if it's really true. Nah!

Don't say anything to yourself or think anything that you would not want someone to say to you — something you wouldn't say to your best friend.

*"You have to have an imaginative mind and tell yourself, 'Hey, I can do whatever I want to."*
*— Torii Hunter*

## TAKE RESPONSIBILITY

Take 100% responsibility for what you are creating out of the experiences that show up. Take ownership for what happens because then you can change it; if it's not your fault, there is nothing you can do about it.

Own responsibility for your responses and for your actions in order to enjoy your best life. Displacing responsibility is giving up your power. Own it, and then do things to support the best possible outcome. Do not let circumstances defeat you.

*"Every problem contains the seeds of its own solution."*
*— Stanley Arnold*

Mistakes are bad, but not learning from them is worse. The key to learning from mistakes is to admit them without excuses or defensiveness. Then make the changes required to grow going forward. If you don't admit your mistakes, you won't grow.

## CREATE AN ANCHOR

An anchor is a tool to reinforce focus. It is a trigger. With a word, or movement, or symbol — or all three — you build belief and motivation, then bring it to the moment whenever you choose. Your brain has a tendency to latch on to anchors which are like mental footnotes. Anchors serve as an energy efficient way to make sense of the world and information around you.

Start by relaxing and imagining images of your success. Feel the good feelings associated with doing well, staying focused, making the play. Amplify the feelings. Then associate it with your anchor (i.e. make a fist pump while saying "Yes!" or just imagine a fist pump). Symbols or pictures are perfect anchors, because just by looking at them, your brain can instantly tap into a certain combination of impulses stored deep in your mind and body. Consider your team logo and using that as an anchor.

Then, during game time or practice, when things get tough, use your anchor to bring you into that feeling of determination and success. Create your anchor to motivate you, then let it evoke a response of relentless perseverance. Work from there.

*"The more frequently two things*
*are experienced together,*
*the more likely it will be that the*
*experience or recall of one*
*will stimulate the recall of the other."*
*— Aristotle*

An anchor conditions you to focus or to get your groove back. Consider creating a response to the other team's cheer or to their crickets (when they go silent in an attempt to mess with your focus).

*"A significant change in behavior is often obvious*
*as the result of a single reinforcement."*
*— Skinner*

## GET PERSPECTIVE

It's never over, till it's over. Every possibility lingers until the final inning is reached and the determining play is made. When everything seems to be going wrong is the time to practice the positive mental belief that you can still achieve your goal. Once you think things are hopeless, you will attract trouble and defeat. Hold the thought that things will shift in your favor. You could win. Or you will lose by less.

Consider this. Bases are loaded and your team is working to shut down the offense. What can you do? Play your part to the best of your ability and inspire your teammates to do the same.

Loaded bases can seem like a daunting problem, or like the perfect opportunity for a double play. Problems and possibilities come from your perceptions. Look at the options. Make clear choices and go after the opportunities.

*NOT OVER TILL OVER* *The score was tied. The opponent was up to bat. Bases loaded and no outs. Defense stood at the ready. The pitch was tossed. The batter swung. HIT! And a low-flying line drive almost hit the dirt as the shortstop scooped it for the OUT then stepped onto second base for the DOUBLE PLAY before the runner could tag-up and continued to chase down and tag the runner who hadn't tagged up at first. TRIPLE PLAY! And the momentum continued as each player got up to bat and scored the winning run. Throughout the game, there is always a possibility for a win — even if the probability is low. Never give up.*

Remember, setbacks pave the way for comebacks. In baseball, as in life, you will not hit every pitch. You will not make every play. So, make the most of the ones you do!

*"Well, that setback sucked;*
*and I just learned how NOT to do it next time."*
*— Unknown*

## OVERCOME

The mind and the body are both involved in every struggle. Every time you meet the challenge, you have the chance to finish stronger than you did the time before. Get the better of it. Prevail.

A bad bounce might beat you in one play. But as long as you pick yourself up and stay in the game, you have a chance. Every battle leads to the next one. Focus completely on this one play. Then on the next one. Win it in the moment and you will see progress in the long haul. The athlete you are today must show up and make the play.

In every play, there is victory and there is defeat. Just as in life, there are times when you overcome and times when you are overcome — mentally or physically. The skill of the opponent, a bad bounce, the heat or cold might get the best of you in a moment. But, as long as you pick yourself up, you'll always have another chance.

Every time you step up to bat, every time you step onto the field, you have the chance to overcome.

---

**player tip** - Arm yourself with positive self-talk. A popular tool for this is to imagine a highlight reel of the greatest plays you've made, the best hits, the times you beat out the throw to the bag. Play it in your mind whenever you require a boost of "I can do this."

Change the stories you tell yourself about the events in your life. Be aware of the difference between the facts in a situation and the way you interpret them. You have a choice about how to view any given event.

Without denying or minimizing the facts, tell the most personally empowering story possible. Recognize how powerfully your story influences what you feel.

*"Nobody likes to get booed... but I know what I can do."*
*— Edgar Renteria*

**coach tip** - Remind players that their job is to get up and play their position to the best of their ability. The results might or might not reflect the work that is done — or it may be an indication of an opportunity to improve. Everybody can learn from the feedback of results. Have the pep talk ready!

*"Our words have the power to lift people up*
*— or put them down.*
*Our words can inspire confidence — or obliterate it.*
*So we must choose our words wisely."*
*— Karen Salmonsohn*

**parent tip** - Mistakes happen. After a game, ask your athlete what they thought about their performance — what did they do well? What struggles did they encounter? What did they learn from it? Did they have fun? And be sure to give them your encouragement.

*"Let developing players make mistakes on the field*
*and help them build their understanding*
*that baseball is a game of failure."*
*— Cameron Bayne*

## LIFE TIP: IT IS OKAY TO MAKE A MISTAKE

Every player — every person — needs to know that it's okay to make mistakes.

Babies make an average of 200 tries before they walk. They *fail* 200 times. Many skills may take 200 or more attempts to get good, or even excellent, at doing. So, there's never really a failure, it's just practice.

Michael Jordan is quoted as saying he missed nine thousand shots, lost 300 games, and was entrusted to make the game-winning shot 26 times where he missed.

Was it more important that he take the shots or not because he was afraid to go for it in case he fell short? He would not succeed without the practice of failure.

*"I've missed more than 9000 shots in my career.*
*I've lost almost 300 games.*
*26 times, I've been trusted to take t*
*he game winning shot and missed.*
*I've failed over and over and over again in my life.*
*And that is why I succeed."*
*— Michael Jordan*

*"Baseball is a game of failure.*
*Make adjustments.*
*Walk the fine line between confident & cocky.*
*Leave the game on the field.*
*Play.*
*Go after it and work hard.*
*You will fail.*
*Believe in yourself.*
*Hustle.*
*Don't throw equipment.*
*Respect the game.*
*Ask questions.*
*You never know who's watching.*
*Friend it out.*
*Take away something every day.*
*Respect elders, parents, coaches.*
*Get your reps in.*
*Get bigger stronger.*
*Grind grind grind.*
*Get consistent.*
*Physical mistakes happen.*
*Mental mistakes, we can fix that.*
*You're gonna fail.*
*Keep improving your game."*
*— Pete Hartmann*

# ELEVEN: BE COACHABLE

As you progress through sports, you will train to get stronger, faster, and you will advance sports-specific skills. You will increasingly learn characteristics such as teamwork and leadership. And, you will respond to being coachable.

Being coachable — what does that mean? It starts with the willingness to be corrected without pushback or defiance. Consider corrections to be feedback. Once you receive the information, give an honest, all-out effort to use that feedback to improve. Accept it as a gift. Don't argue but do ask questions to make sure you understand expectations. Expectations are standards that define daily efforts and behaviors as part of the process to achieving goals.

This skill of being coachable becomes increasingly important, especially if you desire to play at higher levels. Club team coaches, high school coaches, and college coaches seek "coachable" athletes.

*"A coachable athlete is much likelier*
*to reach their potential*
*and is held in high regard by coaches*
*because coachable athletes are easier to teach*
*and they cause a coach less frustration."*
*— Jeff Spelman*

## BEING COACHABLE

It's good to assess your progress in this area and to seek proper guidance if you recognize a problem.

Let's look at aspects of being coachable and identify possible red flags.

## BE RESPECTFUL

Respectful. What does that mean?

> *"Your job as a baseball player is to come to the park*
> *ready to play every day."*
> *— Cal Ripken Jr*

Ask questions, but don't challenge authority — coaches, parents, officials. You may ask a question to learn, but don't defy diretions. That means, don't argue. When your coach calls a play, execute it. When the ump makes a call, accept it. There is a time for questions, but not on the field of play.

> *"Listen to your mom and dad;*
> *they are the ones that want the best for you, regardless."*
> *— Jorge Minyety*

Have a healthy level of respect for the game, teammates, coaches, and officials. Everybody makes mistakes. Some calls are very close, blatantly wrong, even. Let go of the outcome and focus on the next play.

Never ever argue with the umpire. The coaches will contest a call by the umpire if they see a possibility for changing it. Players must keep the focus on the moment. You win some, you lose some.

> *"It ain't nothin' till I call it."*
> *— Bill Klem, umpire*

Be on time. Make sure your gear is ready to go — this includes your uniform, your water jug, your snacks, etc. If your parents are driving you, remind them of the departure time and be ready to go then (that means having your gear loaded in the vehicle). And be sure your head is in the game.

*"Just be ready when they need you."*
*— Dave Concepcion*

Care for your equipment. Respect your glove — never throw it to the ground — that glove could protect you from a line drive to the face one day. Respect your bat — it is a tool to get you on base and all the way home. Do not throw it in anger — toss it correctly after a hit. Respect all of your gear: bag, batting gloves, cleats, batting donut or weights, etc. And be respectful of your teammates' equipment.

Respect your clothing — keep everything clean, tuck in your shirt, wear your hat facing forward.

## BE AN ACTIVE LISTENER

Look the coach in the eye when receiving instruction. Actually hear what is being said, rather than being distracted, disinterested, or defensive.

If you don't understand something, respectfully ask a question to get clarity. If you think you've heard it before, listen again to reinforce it.

---

*HOLD ATTENTION Listen intently and objectively until coach is done talking. Don't walk away in the middle of explanation or directions or reprimand — even if you think you've heard it all before. Listen for something new and let it all sink in for understanding.*

## TAKE RESPONSIBILITY

Look at mistakes objectively. Recognize the choices you made in the situation. Own your contribution, accept consequences, and learn from the experience.

Understand that it's okay to make mistakes. No one will think less of you for admitting an error. In fact, you will earn the respect of others for owning it. When you are confident in your abilities, you won't become defensive when you make a mistake. You will take control of your actions and you gain more control of what happens.

Accepting responsibility and owning your actions gives you personal power in every situation. You see that you have choices. You will learn to make the best ones in support of yourself.

*"If you make it a habit not to blame others, you will feel the growth of the ability to love in your soul, and you will see the growth of goodness in your life."*
*— Leo Tolstoy*

## SHOW IMPROVEMENT

Practice the tough stuff. Do not just practice what comes easy. Take a new skill or concept recently introduced in practice and put it into play during a game (or at least attempt to do it). Step out of your comfort zone and into progressing.

*"Every day, when you go to the field or practice, you can't leave the field the same; you must improve a little bit, every day."*
*— Sundrendy Windster*

When you think "I know this already" let that trigger you to STOP and instead ask yourself "what can I learn from this?" You can always learn a new perspective on something you are familiar with or you might realize that you are not applying it to get the results desired. You may have learned; however, you haven't mastered it, yet.

## MANAGE YOUR EMOTIONS

Behave properly. Do not throw up your arms in the air or huff in frustration when someone corrects you. Realize that feedback is a gift intended to assist your development.

Let go of the outcome. If you strike out or get put out, accept that you did your job to the best of your ability in the moment, and move on. Hustle back to the dugout or to your position and get behind the next play.

If you bobble the ball and the runner makes it on base, complete the play to stop further advancement by the opponent to the best of your ability. Know that you did the best with that experience.

Do not cuss or swear! Foul language is not appropriate and can diminish morale. Take a deep breath, regroup, and keep your composure.

When you meet with triumph, don't gloat. In every case, let go of the result. When you meet with disaster, shake off your frustration and move on to the next battle.

## FOLLOW DIRECTIONS

Be responsive. Always do what the coach says, or at least try. If it doesn't work, you will know you did your job and gave it your best.

Follow the coaches' instructions and don't display selfishness during games by deviating from the game plan and rules. Don't "go rogue" during games.

Your coach calls the shots and it is your job to do what is asked. Get out of the result and stay in the play.

> *"There are 3 types of baseball players:*
> *Those who make it happen,*
> *those who watch it happen,*
> *and those who wonder what happens."*
> — *Tommy Lasorda*

## STAY FOCUSED

Know what is happening at every point of the game. How many outs? How many are on base? Where are the plays? What is the count?

---

*FOCUS vs DISTRACTION Stay focused on the game/practice/ task/lecture at hand. Don't cause a distraction and don't join one (refocus teammates' attention to the game or practice and save other interaction for afterward).*

---

Recognize the difference between having fun and the distraction of messing around. Messing around is not taking it seriously or bumping the hat off your teammate.

Having fun is enjoying the process and the progress. Make the effort to have fun and learn. You can have fun achieving and getting good at your skills. Save the distractions for after practice and after the game.

### SHOW SUPPORT

Encourage your teammates. Never say negative things about them. Remember, everyone makes mistakes. If the last batter made it to first base, and everybody stayed with the play till completed to the best of their ability, move on to the next moment.

If you are injured, suit up, show up, and sit on the bench to support your team. And, remember, the spirit of a baseball team is most important when they are losing rather than when they are winning. Keep up morale.

## BE OPEN MINDED

You don't have to be right. You don't have to know all the answers. Be ready to get feedback and see it as a gift. This means do NOT speak! If you are asked a question, then answer. Otherwise, listen and work.

When you give an explanation that is not asked for, it will appear to be an excuse.

---

*EXCUSES vs EXPLANATION Don't explain unless you are asked, or it sounds like you are making excuses.*

---

## WARNING SIGNS

If you often say or do some of these things, you may struggle with being coachable:

You often say things like:

- "That was not my fault..."
- "Coach picks on me... "
- "I'm not doing that..." (when a coach offers feedback about a technique)

You often do things like:

- Act defensively when receiving instruction (either verbally or through poor body language)

- Blame anyone and anything (teammates, officials, the weather, your equipment, etc.)

- Don't carry out the coach's instructions during a game (instead do as you please)

If you have severe difficult es being coachable, the first place a to look is at self-esteem. Get help. If you cannot take criticism, it's likely because of one thing: You have low self-esteem. It all boils down to a developing a belief that you, by yourself, are enough. Everything else is just experiences to experience.

If you are having a lot of success, that alone doesn't mean you are coachable. At younger ages, greater physical size and an above-average skills (strong arms, fast feet, or other singular skill) may be all you need for success. If you aren't open to change and acquiring higher-level skills, then you may be doomed for less success when you get older (many times at the 12-14 year old age range, or early in high school).

**Final thoughts on being coachable:** Along with a focus on winning, personal accomplishments, and becoming even more competitive, be sure to also consider becoming more coachable. You can be a winner, a fierce competitor, and be coachable, all at the same time. Have respect for yourself and for the game.

**player tip** - Thank your coaches, they work hard to teach you, to encourage you, and to assist you to the next level as an individual and as a team player. Make it a habit to shake hands with them after each practice. Gratitude goes a long way in building your attitude.

**coach tip** - Define expectations repeatedly, and in the simplest terms, among players to ensure clarity. Make sure you are clear about expectations, so you communicate clearly to the players. When possible, let them know why — knowing the intention can help make expectations easier to follow. The lack of clearly understood expectations can be the beginning of poor performance.

> *"Blessed is he who expects nothing,*
> *for he shall never be disappointed."*
> *— Alexander Pope*

**parent tip** - If a your athlete is having severe difficulties being coachable, the first place a to look is at self-esteem. A jaded, overly inflated opinion of abilities and a "know-it- all" mentality can be a mask for insecurity. Don't mistake "confidence" for low self-esteem. Get help.

Want to build self-confidence in your athlete? Catch when they do things right. Notice every little thing that they do well. Underline productive behaviors, actions, and accomplishments. Accept them for who they are and appreciate what they do.

And, heed the words of Shelly Lefkoe: *"No matter what you do, in any situation with your child, ask yourself, What beliefs is my child going to take away from this encounter? Will your child walk away thinking: I just made a mistake and I learned something great or I'm insignificant?"*

There are many opportunities to practice this wise advice.

## LIFE TIP: TAKE RESPONSIBILITY

Here are five facets to taking responsibility for yourself.

**LIVE UP TO YOUR WORD.** Keep your word even when it is difficult, inconvenient, or expensive. Be accountable for your words, actions, and attitude.

**BE DEPENDABLE.** Do what you commit to do. Be reliable — when you agree to do something, do it. If you cannot do it, then own it and revise the promise. You can break your promises and still be in integrity. It's called: renegotiation. Say: I know I made this promise to you. However, I cannot keep it. Here are some other ideas of how I can deliver.

**OWN IT.** Take care of your own business. Don't make others do what you have agreed to do. Take responsibility for your actions. Don't make excuses or blame others.

**THINK THINGS THROUGH.** Use your head. Think before you act — imagine the consequences. Plan ahead.

**SET AN EXAMPLE.** Be diligent. Persevere. Do your best. Have self-control and self-discipline.

*"You owe it to yourself
to be the best you can possibly be
in baseball and in life."*
*— Pete Rose*

*"What you get by achieving your goals
is not as important as what you become
by achieving your goals."*
*— Henry David Thoreau*

*"You have a choice:
You can throw in the towel
or you can use it
to wipe the sweat off your face."*
*— Unknown*

*"It is not about being better than someone else,
it's about being better than you used to be."*
*— Unknown*

*"Every once in a while you come into a situation
where you want to,
and where you have to,
reach down and prove something."*
*— Nolan Ryan*

# TWELVE: PRACTICE

Simply doing the same thing over and over again and expecting to get better, that doesn't work. Be purposeful and deliberate about your practice. Don't get upset at every slip-up. Recognize that it's part of the learning curve. Every master or expert started as a beginner. Remember, practice is how you learn.

*"It is frequent repetition
that produces a natural tendency."*
*— Aristotle*

## HARD TO BEAT

Practice hard, play hard, be hard to beat. Attempting something new, or again, means there is a chance you will struggle. Embrace that because the only way there can be a chance for success is if there is also a chance for failure. Consider that feedback. Adjust and work on it from another angle. Enjoy the process.

*"Practice perfect today,
play like a champion tomorrow."*
*— Unknown*

Before each practice, set well-defined, specific goals for yourself. Create specific intentions for what to improve in this practice session. Identify your long-term goals. Then, break down these goals into mini-goals or baby steps you can take in pursuit of that goal. The small wins help you move toward your Big League goals.

Start every season, every practice with a specific target.

Deliberate practice is focused, intensely focused. Have a plan of action. And, get feedback — from a coach, a parent, or from your results — so you know how you're doing step by step. Immediate feedback assists you in identifying opportunities to improve and areas where you can make adjustments.

When you practice with purpose, it requires getting out of your comfort zone. You must push yourself beyond your comfort zone, beyond what you know, so you will improve.

When you practice, get outside your comfort zone with focus, clear goals, a plan of action, and a way to measure your progress.

Work to develop the proverbial five tools:

1. Hitting for Power
2. Hitting for Average
3. Fielding Ability
4. Throwing Ability
5. Speed

And add Mental Muscle. Get your head in the game. Work on being responsive and resilient. Build your confidence. Commit to doing your best in the moment.

*"A player can have the proverbial five tools*
*and never succeed because his head is not right."*
*— Yogi Berra*

Be the zone, own your experience. Time is an increment of space in which to have an experience — choose how you participate in that increment-how you respond to challenge is how you succeed.

Lots of little things become big changes. Set your sights on improving. Think in terms of a 5% improvement — you could do anything 5% better — but to change something completely is frightening and hard to consider.

*"You'll never be perfect, but you can always
try to find a way to get better;
every single day you can find some way to improve."*
*— Max Scherzer*

Consider that you are developing over the long term. It is about self-improvement and about improving together with your teammates.

*"Baseball is a game of inches."*
*— Branch Rickey*

No matter how terrible or how well yesterday was, today is a new opportunity. Bring your skill set to the field and expect to work with new effort. Every practice gives you a chance to learn something new.

**COMMITMENT**

Lots of things seem to work to improve performance for most people. Almost nothing works for everyone. Approach your performance with commitment and discover what works for you.

*"Only .5% of baseball players will play professionally.
What are you going to do to be part of that .5%?"*

Commit. Be ready to step up under pressure. Practice so that you show up when the clock is winding down. Legends are made of clutch performances exhibited while the game is on the line. Practice creates the habits that support being there in the clutch.

**MECHANICS**

In baseball, as in life, it is essential to get the basics right. Ensuring correct form when you're training prevents injury and allows you to get the most benefit from your effort. Practice basic mechanics constantly.

*"I'm always trying to make sure my
conditioning is all right."*
*— C. C. Sabathia*

## DEVELOP SUPPORTIVE HABITS

Fuel yourself with proper balanced nutrition every day. Do not rely on supplementation to get you over the hump. Do all you can to get adequate sleep nightly, so you recover. Be ready to work as hard as you can every day. Improve at your optimal pace.

*"Never mind what others do; do better than yourself,
beat your own record every day and you are a success."*
*— Speaker W Boetcker*

**player tip** - Behavior-driven triggers support your goals: putting on your uniform in a certain way, arranging bag of gear in a certain way, warming up in a certain way, approaching the batter's box in a certain way, etc. will assist you in establishing and maintaining supportive habits.

Keep a training log to assist you in discovering and developing supportive habits.

*"There's always someone working
just as hard or harder than you,
so days off whether you're mentally
or physically preparing."*
*— Cameron Bayne*

**coach tip** - Remember that a focus on the competitive outcome can sometimes overshadow real improvement. Ask players to look at how far they have come. Encourage them to see the improvements they have made toward their goals. This will motivate them whereas measuring how far they have left to travel will possibly discourage or overwhelm them.

Also, remind players — especially developing athletes who are still growing — to let pain be their guide. If they feel a pinch or a pop or a stab, they should alert you and take action to stretch or rest.

**parent tip** - It is important that your athlete work for improvement and stay within age-appropriate limits. Check with your athlete and with your medical provider regularly to uphold healthy boundaries. Talk with your child about letting pain be a signal that rest is needed. Support them in open and honest communication about what is happening for them.

Recognize when it is time to quit the game completely. When your player's heart isn't in it and when they are no longer having a good time. When the game becomes a burden, not an enjoyment, it is time to move on. There are other things to do that may be more enjoyable and that will inspire your player to achieve the rewards of skill building and excelling.

## LIFE SKILLS — BUILD CONFIDENCE

Self-confidence isn't something we are born with; it is something we develop through achievement. Through practice you build the confidence to achieve your goals.

A lack of confidence is a big mental enemy. Instead of asking "What if this doesn't work?" consider "What if this works?"

Confidence comes from trust, and trust comes from experience. The word "*Confidence*" comes from the Latin word "*Confidero*," which means to trust. Who do you have to trust? Yourself.

Confidence builds with tiny improvements, baby steps. A little progress creates a lot of confidence. You create confidence by having a good practice, by winning a game, not by winning the World Series on day one. You create confidence by having a small success in your life. Then another, and another, and being prepared to weather the inevitable setback.

To trust yourself, you have to gain experience, and in order to gain experience you have to do things over and over and over until you're not even thinking about it anymore. Confidence comes from a positive experience — validation that the repetition is worth it.

Journal it. Write down daily small intentions for improving — remember, small. For example, "Today I'm going to throw 25 pitches to work on my fastball and my changeup," or whatever you are working on.

Write it down and do it. Know that it is something that you can manage. Then, after completing it, return to your journal and write, "Success."

Don't listen to internal voices that try to diminish your efforts. Keep looking at the journal. All you see is successes. With this, you train your brain that you are successful, and you build your confidence.

You are programmed to trivialize your efforts asking "Why are you all excited? That was nothing." Don't buy it. That's your brain programmed to tell you to play it safe. If you buy into that, it's almost guaranteed that you won't be successful at anything. You're never going to be successful if you only focus on what's wrong with you or why you can't do something.

Remember, results often reflect what you THINK will happen — your expectations. Look to the future and aim big. Do not accept limiting thoughts and beliefs about yourself. See yourself as successful. Give yourself encouragement.

When you have confidence, you can play freely instead of holding back. Your ability to believe in your training and to know that you are ready for the game will give you confidence to perform optimally. Knowing and believing that you have done everything possible to prepare gives you a mental edge over the competition, and boosts confidence in your skills and abilities. Confidence allows you to freely apply them.

## CROPS

Build your tool set, nurture success — in baseball and in life.

**Confidence:** recognize every little accomplishment;

**Repetition** — tell yourself "Good Job" every single day;

**Optimism**: find the silver lining in every situation and celebrate it;

**Process**: break down huge, long-term goals into bite size pieces that you can accomplish easily — and this will motivate you to persist;

**Success**: the top dogs in life have gained respect through their work; feeling pride in what you've accomplished leads to dignity and self-respect.

Have an attitude of gratitude. Reflect on your accomplishments with appreciation — for yourself and for what you have done. Recognizing this expansion will assist you in being open to every opportunity.

*"Your education can take you way farther than a football, baseball, track, or basketball will — that's just the bottom line."*
*— Bo Jackson*

*"Baseball is dull only to dull minds."*
*— Red Barber*

*"If you are going to talk the talk, then you have to walk the walk."*
*— Billy Horton*

# THIRTEEN: EDUCATION

The formula for success is: Learn. Do. Repeat.

When you learn something, and you do not apply it, you actually do not really know it — however, because you intellectually understand it, or think you do, you assume you know it. Don't assume it. Apply it.

This is true in life. And it is true in baseball.

Baseball is filled with plays, possibilities, and potentials. It is one facet of your very big life. Build your tool set with Reading, Writing, and Arithmetic plus Music, Art, Science, and Language.

Everything you learn builds upon the other to give you options, ideas, and advantages. A key to success in anything is finding sources of inspiration. Look for stories of those who have been overcome and who have overcome. Athletes, entrepreneurs, artists, etc. can be great teachers for baseball and for life. Explore their stories. And, maybe even, write yours.

Every day is an opportunity to learn about yourself — as an athlete, and as a person. Go the extra mile to experience the growth you desire, and you will know what you require.

And, do what you do for the love of learning in the moment. Statistics show there are 100 to 1 academic vs athletic college scholarships available. If you are truly shooting for a scholarship, you are better off going to the library. If you are fortunate enough to be one of those who earns it playing your sport, the commitment is high. So, you better love the game.

Work hard. Play hard. Be nice. Have fun.

**player tip** - Keep up your grades in school and continue building your physical skill set. Enjoy a range of different adventures to give you the richest life experiences.

**coach tip** - Inspire athletes to take a turn in all positions before they find their specialties and relate instruction to other areas of life when appropriate.

**parent tip** - Encourage your athlete to participate in many different programs and ventures — even if they seem conflicting (for instance, baseball and golf have similarities that could reinforce skills and differences that might build on each other). Make sure they are following their passion, not yours.

# FOURTEEN: LEADERSHIP

As with most things in life, nobody is born a leader. Leaders develop through their own experiences and with support from others. The most important function of a leader is to help great people do great things.

Life is full of smart people and big problems to solve. There is always an opportunity for leaders to step up, to take responsibility for challenges, and to solve them.

## LEADERSHIP

Many times, athletes are looked to for leadership. Strong players or strong personalities can command attention. These teammates are often asked to step into the role of Team Captain.

Being a leader doesn't require a player to be in charge of everyone else, but to lead by example.

- Pay attention.

- Help out.

- Do your best.

- Forgive a mistake — for self and teammates. Cheer on morale.

- Care for yourself and your equipment. Be kind.

Always give yourself and your teammates words of encouragement and reward after a game or practice. Whatever your position, set an example for your teammates to follow. Know your responsibilities and execute with confidence.

**player tip** - Players are often harder on themselves than on one another. Support yourself. Be your own coach. You are your own worst critic and your own best friend. What would you say to a teammate who is feeling discouraged? Be at least that supportive of yourself.

**coach tip** - Lead by example. Be organized and intentional. Spend just five minutes each practice teaching players about leadership to develop a close-knit team in which players are dedicated to growth and success of themselves and their teammates.

Every player on your team is a leader. There are three things a leader can do to lead: Ask someone to do something; Set an example of what to do; Serve or assist someone in their efforts. Players develop leadership skills for on and off the field.

**parent tip** - Lead by example. Show your athlete the power of words. Once you say them, you can't take them back. Many people will remember what you said to them today. And, they will remember how your words made them feel. Use words to inspire, encourage, guide, correct, or soothe. What you say can make someone's day — spread the news.

And, expand that "actions speak louder than words." Remind your athlete that, when combined with positive words, actions show accountability and build trust.

The lesson is that when you combine helpful words with helpful actions you make promises and keep them. This is being a good leader. Keeping promises builds trust. People will believe you and trust you when you keep your word — actually doing what you say you are going to do.

## LIFE TIP: SKILL-BUILDING

Four key tools to up your game.

MOTIVATION: Find out your WHY. We stay motivated when the reasons we choose to do things are specific to us and deeply personal. WHY are you in this game?

SELF-TALK: Retrain your thinking. Every time you entertain a negative thought, counter it with something positive. Be your own best coach.

SELF CONTROL: While you can't control what happens in your life, you can control your reactions to every situation. You can choose to see an unfortunate situation as a minor setback or a complete devastation — it is up to you. Put it in perspective.

VISUALIZATION: Imagine it, and create an epic life. Imagine yourself hitting well, fielding smoothly, base running with stealth, pitching with ease, etc. Watch yourself do it.

Sometimes you've got to see it to believe it, even if the image is all in your head. Close your eyes and visualize yourself executing your best game. It helps build confidence to actually make it happen.

Visualization is proven to help decrease stress or anxiety, improve breathing, and put you in an optimal state of mind to perform your best.

Here's how to do a visualization in three easy steps - **RIP**.

**RELAX.** The more relaxed you are, the more effective your visualization will be. To begin, calm your mind and your body with your breathing. One method is the BOX breath, also called 4x4 breathing: Inhale for 4 seconds, then hold for 4 seconds; exhale for 4 seconds, then hold for 4 seconds. Do 6 to 8 reps.

**IMAGINE.** Relax for the next 5 minutes. With closed eyes, visualize what it feels like to be at your best. Then visualize yourself fielding, throwing, batting, base running. You feel amazing, you're ready for every play. You have laser focus. You are prepared — all of your training and practice has paid off. Your form is impeccable. You feel light on your feet and your breath is in-sync.

Now tap into your senses. See your environment — the dugout, the dirt, the field, the competition. Feel your control, your alertness, your perfect form. Hear the sound of the bat hitting the ball when you are at bat. When you're fielding, see the ball all the way into your glove and then, a perfect play. Throw the ball with speed and accuracy. Hear your breath. See the results.

**PREVAIL.** Mentally overcome obstacles. If there are certain parts of your game that cause you particular concerned, take a moment to visualize conquering those specific spots. Remember to stay focused on the result you desire. Visualize yourself pushing through any potential challenges that may arise during the game. Celebrate your achievement. Open your eyes.

*"Fitness improvement
is about finding the pain free area
and playing there as frequently as possible; you'll notice
the pain free area will expand."*
— *Unknown*

*"If you can't fly then run,
if you can't run then walk,
if you can't walk then crawl, but whatever you do
you have to keep moving forward."*
— *Martin Luther King Jr*

*"You never lose the passion to play."*
— *Sundrendy Windster*

# FIFTEEN: AGILITY

Strength and endurance come from getting fit so you can be useful. Be a protector — protect the plate, protect your base, protect your teammates. Be there for your team. Be energetically fit to be able to bring your best to every play. This is how ordinary players do extraordinary things. Get fit to do your best.

Have some fun getting into shape, staying in shape, and moving on to the next level. Your efforts begin before you start a game or a practice, and end long after the event is over.

*"You use your legs for everything,*
*to field, throw, to hit;*
*it affects everything you do on the field."*
*— Aramis Ramírez*

Get adequate rest. A good night's sleep goes a long way in assisting your body to develop and to recover. Also, schedule days off to rest between workouts. Rest. Repair. Repeat.

Hydrate well. Drink water before, during, after your endeavor or effort. Also, replenish key nutrients along the way — electrolytes and calories are needed to keep your body functioning in top form. Just three percent dehydration can hinder performance.

A good rule of thumb for hydration is to drink half your body weight in ounces every day. So, a 100-pound athlete must drink 50 ounces of water daily. For athletes, it is advised to add fourteen ounces on hot, sweaty days. Athletic drinks can be added after an hour of intense work. Dilute them with water to thwart the gooey flavor.

Fuel your body. Protein, carbohydrates, and fats are all important to keep your body functioning at optimal levels.

Warm up. Before you begin practice or a workout or a game, warm up for activity. Ready all areas that will be called on to make the play. This prepares your body for effort. Extend your muscles till you feel the stretch, but do not strain.

Stretch. Hips, quads, hamstrings, calves, and achilles must be properly stretched. Extend your shoulders and arms and wrists and back and waist. Take a warmup run and get your circulation to assist your readiness. Stretching prepares muscles for effort and helps them recover.

## LET PAIN BE A GUIDE

Respect your body, challenge yourself, but don't go beyond your limits. Lactic acid, soreness, a pop or a pinch tells you that your body requires rest or attention.

Pain can be a welcome adversary. It is, perhaps, our best teacher. Pain signals that we need help.

Seek those who will assist you in finding what caused your pain (or a pop, or discomfort) and determining what comes next.

*At ten years old, he made the All-star team. With a fast bat and a fastball pitch, he brought a lot of skill to the field. Practices were promising. Now it was time for the battle. He was sent to the mound. The energy was high.*

*Wind up. Pitch. STRIKE! Wind up. Pitch. STRIKE! Wind up. STRIKE! One out! Next batter. Wind up. Pitch. STRIKE! Wind up. Pitch. The ball hits the dirt. He looks perplexed. Wind up. Pitch. Ball. Wind up. Pitch. Ball. Wind up. Pitch. Ball.*

*The coaches holler "Throw hard." Dad shakes his head and walks away. Mom looks at him with her quizzical eyes. The coach goes to the mound. He says his arm popped. Does it hurt? No. Okay throw strikes. The coach walks away.*

*He stands on the mound. His body betrays him. His coach abandons him. His parents are disappointed. Occasional strikes are called as he walks three more players, score for the opponent. Finally, the coach replaces him.*

*He walks to the dugout facing all the discouraged stares.*

*Like a caged animal, he paces, not knowing how to deal with the emotional overflow. His mom stands outside the dugout with feckless words of comfort. He hates himself. He hates everyone. He is ten years old. He throws his glove. He gets a reputation as a hothead.*

*Diagnosed with little league shoulder, he spends eight weeks to rest and four weeks to rehab. He returns to pitch and his shoulder pops. Any pain? No. But, the coach advises, check out the pop, anyhow.*

*Turns out to be Loose Shoulder. The muscle out- developed the skeletal structure.*

*His body didn't abandon him, it saved him — by not responding when he was throwing pitches with such strength that his arm popped out of the shoulder socket (and fortunately back in place), threatening greater injury.*

*So, eight more weeks of recovery and rehab. He grows out of the shoulder issues. And still he struggles with the emotional trauma of that season.*

---

Pain can be a good sign. It signals when you have pushed your limits — within reason, or beyond what is healthy. Expand your comfort zone, and you will achieve pain as a result. To let pain be your guide you have to understand the pain.

*"To push the boundaries,*
*you need to know where the edges are."*
*— Mark Boulton*

A gradual lengthening and strengthening feeling that is uncomfortable, hurts, but it's a dull, soft pain is a sign you are challenging your body. This is a pain you can mentally bare. This pain is for your growth and physical transformation.

However, a sharp, sudden ache is your body signaling that you have gone beyond your abilities of that moment. You have gone too far — way beyond your comfort zone. Know your limitation and slightly go beyond it. Don't overdo it.

In attempts to rid pain, many seek that which would help mask it. It is tempting, however, think bigger. Recognize that pain will always return until it is correctly managed.

Accept the pain. Deal with it appropriately. Then move forward. You can't keep throwing if your elbow is in pain. You need to stop, address your pain, and then do something else (at least for a while). You train so you can do more. That doesn't mean it has to hurt.

When you are recuperating from an injury, find alternative ways to improve your game. What step can you take that doesn't hurt that also moves you towards your goal? Do that; play there... get comfortable. Then... look for what's next!

In the off season take time to reset by training your core and total body in a different way. Return to perfect posture and build alignment after overuse of the same muscles used during the season of play. Agility is not inexhaustible. Your ability to move quickly builds over time. Allow your body to rest, reset, and realign so you can build again.

RESET: Rest, Evaluate, Sleep, Eat, Train

**player tip** - Consider keeping a log of your practices and workouts. Add insight about how you felt, what worked, what was tough. This will fortify your efforts, and, it will be a great way to relive your journey. And, it will help keep you on track with your workouts.

Remember, always break up hard workout days with a day of light work or rest. Repeat skill development lessons in a variety of ways — drills, exercises, reading, watching, envisioning, journaling, etc. Be dedicated to learning and improving.

**coach tip** - Encourage players to take a day off — or at least to alternate activity — maybe a leisurely swim, a good stretch, or a relaxing hike in nature for a change of pace. A recovery day of rest or a light workout is important to building strength and endurance.

**parent tip** - Support your athlete with the right regimen. Spend time reading about nutrition with your player — get them involved in discovering fortifying foods that they enjoy. Time in the kitchen could lead to healthy eating habits that last a lifetime.

# PLEASE REMEMBER:

1. THESE ARE KIDS.
2. THIS IS A GAME.
3. COACHES ARE VOLUNTEERS.
4. UMPIRES ARE HUMAN.
5. YOU DO NOT PLAY FOR THE YANKEES.

*Thank you*

## LITTLE LEAGUE
# BASEBALL

# SIXTEEN: EQUIPMENT

Maintain the integrity of your equipment. You've invested in choosing and purchasing your baseball equipment. Take care of it. Properly storing your equipment when it's not in use will keep it in great shape when you need it.

## BASEBALL BATS

Low temperatures — weather cooler than 60 degrees Fahrenheit — can cause the density of a bat to change, causing the bat to become brittle and prone to cracks and dents.

Low temperatures can also cause baseballs to become harder, which could also cause more damage to a baseball bat. So be mindful of when you're using your baseball bat when the weather's chilly.

Storing your bat correctly can also help it last longer. Do not throw your baseball bat in the garage during the winter; keeping it away from extremely hot or extremely cold temperatures is imperative. Cover your bats with a bat sleeve if you have more than one so they don't clash against each other.

Wipe down the barrel of your bat to remove the dirt and keep it smooth. Avoid dents by rotating the bat after each hit. When it's not in use, store your bat vertically with the barrel facing down.

## BASEBALL GLOVES

Baseball gloves are personal. Your glove almost becomes an extension of your hand when you catch the ball. Generally, players under the age of 12 will use a glove in the 10-11 inch range, while older players will use a glove between 11 and 13 inches.

Break it in. Playing catch is the best way to break in a new glove, but when you're learning, use a glove that's not brand new.

Make sure the leather is broken in enough that you can easily open and close the glove. If you can't squeeze shut your glove, it'll be tough to hold on to the ball.

The catcher's glove is not the only one that has a unique style. As players specialize, there are gloves for different positions. For instance, first base glove is fashioned to assist in scooping or picking the ball. An infielder's mitt might be lightweight to assist in responding quickly to a hard hit ball.

Store your glove between games and practices on a shelf at room temperature or in a cool, dark place. Do not store your glove outside, in your equipment bag, or near a heater.

Keep your glove dry. If it gets wet, wipe it with an absorbent, clean rag and then let it air dry. After use in games or practice, wipe down your glove with a clean rag to get rid of dirt or debris. Store it in a cool, dry place daily.

Gloves can maintain their longevity if cared for properly, however they do require some upkeep to stay in top shape.

END OF SEASON: Before storing your glove at the end of the season, do a quick once-over to determine any needed repairs. Doing them at the end of the season is much easier than at the beginning of next season.

Oiling your glove is something you could consider doing to break it in or before storing it for the season. Leather glove oil, conditioners, and cleaners are available specifically for baseball gloves, however, some alternatives that might work include petroleum jelly, baby oil, or saddle soap. The glove manufacturer or sporting goods store will likely have a recommendation for products that have worked best.

Some players do not like using oil or conditioners on gloves believing it will deteriorate the leather faster or make the glove heavier. Much of this is a personal preference.

Be sure to let the glove fully dry after oiling or cleaning it and before tightening the laces and putting it in storage.

## BASEBALLS

Store them in a bucket or bin so they don't roll away and become lost. Notice when they are getting dried out and frayed. Loose threads and tears in the leather will affect performance of the ball in throwing and hitting and fielding.

The stitching that holds together the covering of the baseball is a significant characteristic. The stitches are slightly raised and catch the wind. Like wings on a plane, the stitches cause the ball to move — swerving sharply or gradually, right or left, downward, or a combination of moves, depending on which direction, and how fast, the pitcher puts a spin on the ball. So, any debris, fray, or blemish on the ball will affect performance. Keep them in good shape and store them properly.

## CLEATS

Keep your cleats clean. Keep the leather clean and dry; and keep spikes free of dirt to prolong their use.

## CATCHER'S GEAR

Keep your gear clean. Like with your glove, brush off dirt and mud after each use. A catcher's gear gets a lot of wear and tear. Clean your gear to prolong its use.

Here are some items useful for cleaning and maintaining catcher's equipment: shoe brush, glove oil, leather laces, re-lacing tool, soft rag.

Shin Guards: Make sure the straps are not worn or frayed, adjust them to fit correctly. Check strap hooks and replace any that are damaged or broken.

Chest Protector: Air out your chest protector after use. Check straps — keep them untwisted and protect your hook/clasp. If needed, replace damaged clasps.

Face Mask and Helmet: Check straps for wear and ensure your mask fits snuggly — not too tight or not too loose. Check for cracks — a cracked helmet should be replaced immediately.

## BASEBALL BAG

While you are in-season you should keep your equipment in a bag big enough to hold everything you require. There are specialized bags for catchers. During the off-season, store your equipment out of extremely dry or damp places.

## PROTECTIVE GEAR

Cup, mouth guard, shin guards, kneepads and other protective devises should be cared for appropriately. Make sure they are ready to work with you next season!

---

**player tip** - Create a habit of putting away your equipment in a certain way. This will assist you in caring for everything, and in keeping track of it all.

**coach tip** - Remind players to respect equipment of teammates. Sharing is often part of the game, and in that, instruct players to be respectful when borrowing equipment. Reinforce this message.

Ensure proper equipment for your players. The correct type of cleats, correct size glove (and how to break in a glove), and the use of protective gear like cups and mouthpieces.

**parent tip** - Assist your player in getting the correct gear, teach them how to care for it, and give them responsibility for caring for all of it.

## CROPS

Here is another chance to pull the weeds and plant the seeds of supportive habits.

**Confidence**: write down a skill you are building in the form of an affirmation, for instance "I have laser focus on the ball so I can field it every time," and say it aloud to yourself — feel it; do this every day until you are convinced it is true;

**Repetition**: learn new stuff in at least six different ways, then repeat them for mastery — cycling information is key to learning as every time you hear it or experience it again, you deepen your understanding of it;

**Optimism**: focus on your desired result, think of how you would like things to turn out and fill your mind with thoughts of success, then let it unfold;

**Process**: keep joy of playing the game part of every developmental stage;

**Success**: define your successful season based on your goals for improvement (and that isn't always reflected by win/loss records).

*"Tell me and I forget;*
*teach me and I may remember;*
*involve me and I will learn."*
*— Confucius*

# SEVENTEEN: HUDDLE

After the top and bottom of each inning, it is typical to huddle for review, reflect É what worked, what didn't. This is a great time to provide feedback, share lessons learned, and encourage the team for the next moment.

Summarize the team's activity. Give praise for what went well. Be specific and recognize progress. Discuss opportunities for improvement. Clarify expectations. When appropriate, note any humorous thing that happened. And, no public criticism; when necessary, take a player aside.

## PRAISE IN PUBLIC, REPRIMAND IN PRIVATE

As in life, it is important not to demean players' value by publicly reprimanding them. Often, coaches (and bosses, and teachers, and etc.) feel that public scolding sets an example for everyone else. While this may be the case, it typically creates more harm than good.

Public criticism is humiliating and embarrassing to the player. It erodes team morale for all who witness it. And, it sets up conflict.

Take it aside, in private. Whatever the end result is of the reprimand, it is not for other teammates to know. Reprimanding in private allows the resolution to remain private as well.

Keep calm. Possibly the most important reason to reprimand in private is that the act of removing player and coach from the situation gives both an opportunity to calm down and then address the issue with composure.

Baseball is like a microcosm of the human experience. Players are full of flaws, subject to doubt, and asked to bring their best even in the worst pressure-filled situations. In every area of life, it is important to uphold dignity.

Taking the time to step back (as with assessing a fly ball to the outfield), get calm, and discuss issues in private will build loyalty and trust. It will also increase morale, allowing athletes to feel comfortable approaching coaches with issues, and stave off potential outbursts or awkward situations with teammates, fans, or stakeholders. Anybody who hears the message or anyone who overhears it will form an impression.

Whether the ball lands true or takes a bad bounce, in baseball, like in life, success is about resilience. It's about responding under pressure, about making the best of the situation, and about moving on.

As in life, each baseball player must find the way to fit in and to stand out by doing well, physically and emotionally. Balance comes from moving forward in life productively, pro-actively, and on purpose with purpose. Be the one person in your life who makes a difference.

## AFTER THE GAME

Over many years and with many athletes from all levels — when asked what is your worst memory from playing sports, the overwhelming response was "the ride home."

---

**MEMORIES:** *Hundreds of college athletes were asked to think back: "What is your worst memory from playing youth and high school sports?"*

*Their overwhelming response: "The ride home from games with my parents."*

*The informal survey lasted three decades, initiated by two former longtime coaches who over time became staunch advocates for the player, for the adolescent, for the child. Bruce E. Brown and Rob Miller of Proactive Coaching LLC are devoted to helping adults avoid becoming a nightmare sports parent.*

*Those same college athletes were asked what their parents said that made them feel great, that amplified their joy during and after a ballgame. Their overwhelming response: "I love to watch you play."*

*— Steve Henson*

---

*In baseball, and in life, too often parents (and other authority figures) provide more advice than approval. The athlete requires time and space to recover, to process their experience. Save your analysis of the game, their performance, the coaches, umpires, and other players. Let them bring the game to you and enjoy watching them play — not just watching them win.*

*Tell your child "I love watching you play." This lets them know that their value is not tied to their performance and it gives them confidence to take risks, manage failure, and grow.*

*Like baseball, LIFE is a game. The goal is to have an extraordinary enjoyable experience, day by day. Steal the fullness of life. Move forward toward your dream.*

*Whatever you do, the little things become habits...habits that fuel your performance and assist you in focus. Focus means you are engaged, energized, and optimally effective in the role you choose to experience.*

---

**player tip** - It's not your job to hold everyone accountable — you are only responsible for yourself. Take ownership of your own mistakes.

You can't fix it if you don't own it. Always look for greatness in yourself. It's there. And the mistakes keep making you stronger. You do the best you can. And then you learn and you do better.

Play for yourself. Realize that your athletic performance does not define who you are; it is just another dimension of your experiences. Remember, your performance is just that — your performance.

171

**coach tip** - Feedback is important. And, so is dignity. Take on the compassionate role to enable your team to strive collectively for higher levels of success. When dealing with members of the team who have issues, always show willingness to understand the situation before taking action. The need of the moment is to respond and not react. When the focus is on the response rather than reaction, there is time to evaluate various factors, especially the consequences and impact of the response. Remember to shower athletes with praises in public, and when issues occur, reprimand in private.

How you deal with mistakes is important in the development of an athlete. Never demean a willing learner. You don't want your players to play fearfully. You want them to play fearlessly and you want them to be willing to take risks. You don't want them to focus on playing self-consciously because they don't want you to react.

Most athletes fear making a mistake, letting down their team, or not making "the" play that causes the team to lose. By understanding that athletes will make mistakes, allowing them to make mistakes — and to learn from those mistakes — you assist athletes to lose their fear and then they can play a more focused, fearless game.

You don't always have to correct the obvious (they know if they swung at a pitch in the dirt that it was a bad pitch). Be encouraging. Let them know that their value isn't dependent on the win or the loss.

**parent tip** - Emotions can get the best of us. Think carefully before you communicate a message when you are emotional. A good message can turn bad when it's done wrong. Help your athlete own their blunders and then assist in restoring their honor. We all make mistakes.

If you are hollering at an official or taking a loss harder than the players, you are not allowing your child to have their own experience.

Release your athlete to the team and to the coach (as long as it is a safe environment). Trust the experience to them, allowing your child to take risks and develop their own instincts.

## LIFE TIP...GET IN THE GAME

According to T Harv Eker, motivational speaker known for his theories on wealth and motivation, the most important thing you can do in your entire life, whatever you do, is to get in the game. When it comes to success, in life, in sports, in your career endeavors, it is critical to play. Put things in motion.

You can practice, you can prepare, you can watch baseball, you can get the gear and put on the baseball uniform, you can warm up. But that's preparing. You gotta get in the game.

You learn faster and better by being in the game — by actually doing — versus just thinking about it and preparing for it. While you're in the game, you have to adjust to the circumstances, make corrections, let go of mistakes, stay in the moment. It's when practice comes together in the real world.

...And, change things up. Experience everything. Play baseball during baseball season and play something else once in a while. Everybody gets better with a vacation.

So go out there and pursue your big league dreams. With grit, you will find growth. No dream is too big if your heart is in it. This is your life. Game on!

*"I don't believe a player is ever a finished product."*
*— Anthony Rizzo*

TK Lynn

*"If there was magic in this world,
it happened within sight of the
three bases and home plate."*
— *Tee Morris*

# ABOUT THE AUTHOR

*T. K. Lynn is an author, a screenwriter, a strategic creative director, and a life artist living in Scottsdale Arizona where baseball is played year-round. Always be curious and you will always be delighted. Play ball!*

www.ingramcontent.com/pod-product-compliance
Lightning Source LLC
Chambersburg PA
CBHW031621040426
42452CB00007B/619